Publish or Perish: The Wrong Issue

Leslie H. Cochran

AGENDAS
ALTERNATIVES
APPLICATIONS
ACTIONS

ISBN 0-9631438-1-6

Library of Congress card number: 91-091555

Printed in the United States of America

Library of Congress Cataloging-in-Publication Data

Cochran, Leslie H., 1939-

    Publish or Perish: The Wrong Issue
    Bibliography: p. 167

  1. Education, Higher -- United States
  2. College Teaching -- United States
  3. Learning and Scholarship -- United States

  I. Title

StepUp
incorporated
Publications Division
2 Spanish Street Court
Cape Girardeau, Missouri 63701
Telephone (314) 334-8034

CONTENTS

APPLICATIONS

ACTIONS

Preface

The publish or perish controversy has been a source of growing debate throughout the last third of this century. For the most part, however, the debate has centered on an "either/or" proposition rather than addressing ways to resolve the conflict. While much has been said about this issue, campus-based initiatives have been limited and had little or no lasting impact.

Publish or Perish: The Wrong Issue is focused directly on this problem. It is designed as a means to translate the rhetoric of the past into action for the future. It establishes a theoretical base and delineates the issues that must be addressed. Rather than lamenting the current situation, it provides tangible examples to guide campus leaders in answering the real questions:

- How can teaching and scholarship be integrated?
- How can a broader definition of scholarship be implemented?
- How can what professors actually do be used to elevate their professional competence?
- What is the proper balance between teaching and scholarship?
- What alternative measures can be used to elevate teaching, learning, and scholarship?
- What actions can be taken by campus leaders to enhance the role of teaching?

Responses to these questions require the professoriate to probe existing priorities. They demand a willingness to question existing values and to expose some sacred cows. They require the development of a teacher scholar model that integrates teaching and scholarship. They force the reassessment of current thinking and the development of new approaches to evaluation. And finally, they call for strong action-oriented leadership that is committed to translating teacher scholar theory into action.

The work for this book started in 1987 with a national survey of chief academic officers. Over 1300 colleagues responded to this study which was published in 1989 as **Administrative Commitment to Teaching.** During the last two years, the insights and ideas generated in the initial research have been refined. I am deeply indebted to my many friends who tolerated the lectures, questioned the theory, and helped refine the concepts presented in this publication. I want to express a special gratitude to my colleagues who read chapters once, twice, and on a few occasions three times--Dorothy Allen, Charles Bonwell, Sheila Caskey, Pauline Fox, Robert Hamblin, Thomas Harte, Ernest Kern, and Jane Stephens. Without the help of these colleagues at Southeast Missouri State University, the manuscript would have probably ended in the trash container. I appreciate, too, the special advice given by my longstanding friends, James Eison, at the University of South Florida, and James Scanlon, at Clarion University of Pennsylvania.

In addition, there is a long list of faculty colleagues at Southeast Missouri State University who drafted essays dealing with the application of the teacher scholar approach to their discipline. I want to extend a special thanks to Peter Bergerson, Shelba Branscum, Michael Brown, Sheila Caskey, William Chamberlain, Jennie Cooper, Sterling Cossaboom, Anthony Duben, Pauline Fox, Peter Gordon, Robert Hamblin, Thomas Harte, Dennis Holt, Charles Ireland, Ernest Kern, Michael Readnour, Sandra Renegar, Keith Russell, Robert Sheets, Alice Strange, and Janet Weber. I really appreciate their willingness to rethink the process. And finally, I want to give a special commendation to Deborah Blumenberg. Somehow she was able to translate the scribbled notes into meaningful sentences and to perfect the sections into a readable manuscript. Without the help of all of these colleagues, the completion of this book would not have been possible.

L.H.C.

Agendas

Premise

Change requires the willingness to challenge the status quo.

Challenge

To facilitate open discussion, one must:
- Analyze current values
- Question existing practices
- Be willing to replace outdated policies

CHAPTER 1

ADDRESSING THE REAL ISSUES

The publish or perish controversy has been a source of growing debate throughout the last quarter of this century. For the most part, however, the debate has been cast as a question of "either/or" rather than attempting to address substantive means of resolving the real and perceived conflicts. Only during the student protest years of the sixties and seventies was the concern over the quality of teaching elevated beyond its normal role in the teaching, research, and service triad. Like many other concerns of the time, the importance of teaching and its interrelationships with scholarly research dissipated and soon became another casualty in higher education's unfinished revolution. In more recent years the academy, again, has witnessed a substantial increase in the rhetoric aimed at resolving the tensions between teaching and research. This time there is one major difference. Numerous national leaders--Alexander W. Astin, Ernest L. Boyer, K. Patricia Cross, Russell Edgerton, and John I. Goodlad to mention a few --have called for reform that places greater emphasis on the various aspects of teaching. Still, the academy has been relatively complacent and has continued largely in a business-as-usual manner.

To reflect briefly on the history of American higher education, it is easy to understand why changes have occurred in such a lethargic manner. The changing educational needs of our culture have evolved in response to social, economic, and political conditions. As a result, the educational outcomes desired have shifted from an emphasis on learning facts, to developing skills, and, more recently, to understanding concepts. Similarly, the modes of instruction have evolved from a passive to a more active learning base. The nature of the profession has moved from an intellectual development framework (which may be called character development to reflect the Jeffersonian ideal of a college education) to an emphasis on professional development. The same general movement can be seen in the overall educational theme which has progressed from a transmission of knowledge to a greater level of attention being focused on the facilitation of learning.

While one might argue with the precise description of these phases and how they are characterized, it is clear that higher education has been in a steady process of evolutionary change. As shown by Chart 1, the paralleling shifts from scholar to research scholar and finally to teacher scholar can be readily followed. Although these illustrations represent broad generalizations, they suggest that the profession is currently at a major point of demarcation. Within this context, the ferment of the nineties can be clearly projected. Regardless of the reasoning, the issues that must be faced will likely be most traumatic for a large segment of the professoriate. The challenge is to move institutions that have become firmly entrenched in the values of the twentieth century (industrial age) into the twenty-first century (information age).

Chart 1
Evolutionary Nature of Higher Education in America

Century	Dominant Faculty Theme	Major Faculty Characteristic	Basic Educational Theme	Primary Instructional Modes	Foremost Educational Outcome
19th	Intellectual Development	Scholar	Transmission of Knowledge	Passive Learning	Learn Facts
20th	Research Development	Research Scholar	Generation of Knowledge	Problem Solving	Develop Skills/Abilities
21st	Professional Development	Teacher Scholar	Facilitation of Learning	Active Learning	Understand Concepts

It is obvious, then, that during a part of our nation's history, it may have been easier to justify the existence of a singular thrust in teaching or research. The pace of college life was different. The expectations of faculty were fewer and the public and students were far less demanding. While some faculty members today long for the days when they felt that teaching was their only obligation, on most campuses those days are gone. The knowledge explosion and the needs of society have extended the need for continuous, ongoing scholarship. The complexities of the modern campus have virtually eliminated the singularly-minded teaching professor. Gone, too, on most campuses, is the position of the highly productive researcher who has little skill or time to fulfill teaching responsibilities. Economic

The issues that must be faced will likely be most traumatic for a large segment of the professoriate. The challenge is to move institutions that have become firmly entrenched in the values of the twentieth century (industrial age) into the twenty-first century (information age).

and employment conditions simply do not allow that type of circumstance. Furthermore, students commonly do not tolerate such classroom indifference.

Today's expectations have produced conditions experienced by most senior faculty members that are very different than when they entered the profession. Even those who entered the profession in the last decade sense the changing character of the academy. It can be expected that these value shifts will be even more dramatic in the decades ahead. Other changes that are emerging in the academic work environment will compound this situation and likely create a totally new context for the professoriate in the century ahead. While many are currently unwilling to accept the eighties as the good years, faculty members will begrudgingly find that in comparison to the ferment of the nineties, it will likely be the best decade they can recall. Salary increases that parallel inflation will sound good. Tinkering with assessment measures will seem passé. The lack of workload accountability measures will be a remote part of history. And for those unable to adjust, the concern over morale issues will become even more unbearable.

While many are currently unwilling to accept the eighties as the good years, faculty members will begrudgingly find that in comparison to the ferment of the nineties, it will likely be the best decade they can recall.

For those sensitive to the overall direction of higher education, the challenge to focus attention on our primary responsibility, "creating intellectual activity that stimulates teaching and learning," will become even greater. It is from this holistic perspective that teaching, learning, and scholarship will become an integral whole. **This process thereby defines faculty members as teacher scholars.** It forms an integrated continuum where the various forms of scholarship complement teaching, teaching fosters continued scholarship, and learning naturally flows from these relationships.

While the professoriate commonly supports much of this philosophical position, the practical procedures to facilitate this conceptualization are all-too-often woefully lacking. Contradictions between theory and practice abound! The essential work of teaching maintains the system. It provides an unsurpassed avenue for intellectual discourse and debate. Teaching serves as a great source of intrinsic satisfaction and produces intense commitment from many academics. While prestige often comes from scholarly research and publications, most faculty members prefer teaching. The vast majority of academics across the nation want to do some research, publish a little, and maintain teaching as their first love. (5) Yet, the system is not designed to support, reward, or promote this type of behavior. The blame for this dilemma must be shared by all, but the burden for change must be assumed by faculty members and administrators alike. Faculty members themselves must assume a proactive role in addressing the real issues and devising alternative structures. Administrators must stimulate the debate and find ways to implement the changes.

The message for higher education is clear. The decade of the nineties presents an opportunity for reform. Some would exhort this change to occur overnight in a revolutionary manner, but the likelihood of this occurrence is remote. In reality, a shift of this magnitude will only occur in an evolutionary manner. Indeed, many of the necessary elements to integrate teaching and scholarship are not currently in place on many campuses. Work needs to be completed on various employment procedures, evaluative alternatives, reward systems, and most importantly, changes must be forthcoming in the attitudes that prevail throughout the profession. This transformation will not happen overnight, nor will the changes occur easily. It will require a resolve to debate the issues, to understand current research, to propose new evaluative strategies, and to construct procedures and policies that implement the new emphasis. Most of all, it will require a strong commitment to reorder current priorities and practices.

The system is not designed to support, reward, or promote this type of behavior.... Faculty members must assume a proactive role in addressing the issues and devising alternative structures. Administrators must stimulate the debate and find ways to implement the changes.

It is commonly recognized that the profession gives tremendous lip-service support to the primacy of teaching. Teaching is the preferred activity of over two-thirds of the faculty members across the nation. (2) But when it comes to rewards, the value of teaching is deflated. Continuing discussion of the publish or perish syndrome is counter productive. Indeed, publish or perish is the wrong issue! This dilemma cannot be dismissed in a haphazard fashion, nor can it be set aside as some philosophical perspectives that are beyond response. The demands for change are real and must be addressed in a rational manner. The time has come for the professoriate to address the real issues.

THE REAL ISSUES

- How can teaching and scholarship be successfully integrated?

- How can a broader definition of scholarship be implemented?

- How can what professors actually do be used to evaluate their professional competence?

- What is the proper balance between teaching and scholarship?

- What alternative measures can be used to evaluate teaching, learning, and scholarship?

- What actions can campus leaders take to enhance the role of teaching?

It is these very questions and corresponding challenges that present a realistic context for this book. The chapters that follow progress in a step-by-step fashion to reveal existing shortcomings; to suggest new responses to some age-old questions; to provide new ways of thinking about the assessment and evaluation processes; and, then, to present a series of action-oriented approaches designed specifically to stimulate the reform process.

As a starting point, Chapter 2 identifies a series of value conflicts and sacred cows that must be faced. The existence of these perspectives and perceptions cannot be ignored. Chapter 3 provides a rationale for the development of a philosophical framework. A teacher scholar model that integrates teaching and research is proposed, a broader definition of scholarship is suggested, and an expanded evaluation base for teaching is delineated. Chapter 4 develops these concepts into a teacher scholar model. Specific attention is focused on connecting what faculty members actually do with how they are evaluated and rewarded. Chapter 5 translates this model into action. It provides a broadened base for evaluating scholarship and proposes alternative approaches to the traditional evaluative measures and rewards in current use. Chapter 6 is designed to suggest new ways of thinking about the assessment process. Essays from faculty members in different disciplines are used to illustrate various alternatives to the traditional "publishing validation process." In Chapter 7, the campus change process is subdivided into five major areas and numerous examples are provided on how the change initiative might be facilitated. These are supplemented by literally hundreds of ideas that might be used in campus-based workshops. Finally, in Chapter 8 a series of leadership challenges are provided to suggest directions for the future. Leadership challenges and guiding principles for the change process are suggested for the key change agents--administrators, department chairpersons, and faculty members.

The overall design of the book is intended to shift the attention of the profession to the "nitty gritty" of how to bring about the required reform. It establishes a theoretical base and then raises a set of issues that must be addressed. If the emphasis on teaching is to move forward in an constructive manner, action-oriented steps must be taken. Specific answers must be forthcoming. Tangible alternatives must be proposed. Strong leadership must be present. The fundamental intellectual processes inherent in academic pursuit must now be applied to the profession itself.

If the emphasis on teaching is to move forward in an aggressive manner, action-oriented steps must be taken. . . . Strong leadership must be present. The fundamental intellectual processes inherent in academic pursuit must now be applied to the profession itself.

These ideals form the basis for a reform effort that moves beyond the narrow confines of the present publish or perish debate. The reform requires strong, dynamic leadership that builds upon the four major premises of this book:

- **Change requires the willingness to challenge the status quo.**

- **Change depends upon new alternatives being presented.**

- **Change encourages those involved to rethink the process.**

- **Change requires leadership that is action-oriented.**

CHAPTER 2

EXPOSING THE HIDDEN CONSTRAINTS

The context in which change occurs presents a number of constraints and challenges. Often the associated tangible and intangible beliefs, values, attitudes, and myths have considerable affect on the change process itself. An initial step, therefore, in any such effort must be to openly debate such commonly held perceptions. Whenever possible, the negative aspects of these concerns need to be set aside. When this is not possible, the issues at least need to be exposed and dealt with in a constructive manner. Clearly, the current perceptions of teaching and research present numerous dilemmas that impact and may impede any substantive change in the status quo. In this chapter, some of the most basic value conflicts and sacred cows are exposed as reminders of the real world in which change must occur.

As already suggested, the questions to be answered are relatively simple. They raise, however, fundamental issues that have roots firmly entrenched in some of higher education's most long-standing traditions. The reform also targets the current status given to research. While more recent in its evolution, it, too, is clearly established as one of the academy's sacred cows (if not its cash cow). Pervasive as these challenges might be, the complexity of the task fails to provide sufficient rationale for not pursuing the reform initiative. There must be a willingness to debate all issues and consider new perspectives!

Facing the Value Conflicts

While teaching is the most fundamental intellectual pursuit on college campuses, it also produces the most obvious value conflict. It has often been one of two competing priorities which has resulted in a mismatch between myth and reality. The teaching/learning process is the essence of what an institution of higher learning is all about, but somehow the manner in which these activities are practiced, nurtured, and rewarded leaves much to be desired. Faculty members at most institutions devote the vast majority of their time to the instructional process, and yet, these efforts are seldom fully rewarded. Providing appropriate rewards is often identified by faculty members as the first step toward establishing a balanced perspective between the importance of teaching and research. While faculty members cite the need for immediate changes in existing reward structures, other equally important changes must be implemented before significant adjustments are made in terms of rewards. Initiatives need to be taken that establish new instructional effectiveness data bases, create expanded evaluation procedures, and facilitate in-class peer and administrative review of teaching activities. Current interest in evaluation must be significantly enhanced if teaching is to be elevated to the apex of the academic value structure. New attitudes and actions to reinforce these changes must become commonplace before the required reward structures can be implemented. The faculty goal of increased rewards will not occur until documentable evidence of teaching becomes available.

The teaching/learning process is the essence of what an institution of higher learning is all about, but somehow the manner in which these activities are practiced, nurtured, and rewarded leaves much to be desired. . . . The faculty goal of rewards will not occur until documentable evidence of teaching becomes available.

A second remarkable anomaly of American higher education is the absence of internal and external measures of institutional and social accountability. Some individuals in the profession are insulted whenever questions are raised about the quality of programs, the effectiveness of instruction, or their productivity as faculty members. While part of the larger reform movement, the question of accountability looms so large on the college teaching agenda that it deserves special attention. There is widespread skepticism about the current quality of higher education. There is a public sense that academic standards are too low. There are demands from state legislatures to measure student learning outcomes. There are ongoing debates within the professoriate regarding program review, outcomes assessment, and the evaluation of teaching. Society, in general, has very little understanding of the academy, and respect for its accountability is dwindling.

There are conflicts, too, on how teaching and scholarship are treated at different types of institutions. The type of institutional designation (which I detest)--"research" or "teaching"--should have no bearing on how teaching or research is stimulated. Of course, a land grant institution has a significant obligation to support scholarly activity, but it has the same responsibility as all other institutions to support teaching. Boyer vividly emphasized this point when he called for equal treatment of both.

> *At the same time research institutions also must aggressively support good teaching. After all, at large universities, where much of the research is conducted, two-thirds or more of all students are undergraduates, and the push to publish, without an equal concern for teaching, can have a chilling effect on the classroom and be shockingly detrimental to the students.*

> *We conclude then that, at every research university, teaching should be valued as highly as research, and good teaching should be an equally important criterion for tenure and promotion. To expect faculty to be good researchers and good teachers is a demanding standard. Still, it is at the research university where the two come together, and faculty, at such institutions, should contribute effectively to both. (3:126)*

All institutions run this same risk of letting certain institutional priorities (values) overly influence those of the professoriate. There are different reasons for scholarship, depending on which perspective one might espouse -- institutional or individual. The faculty reward structure must function within an institutional context, but focus on instructional priorities.

There are different reasons for scholarship, depending on which perspective one might espouse--institutional or individual. The faculty reward structure must function within an institutional context, but focus on instructional priorities.

Within the academy, there is a long list of other value conflicts. Rather than dwelling on all of them, it might suffice to mention only a few. 1) A campus visit or review of an institution's promotional publicity always brings forward clear accolades about the importance of teaching, but a deeper probing seldom reveals tangible indicators of such instructional effectiveness. 2) Research and creative endeavors defined as purposeful intellectual activity are legitimate expectations for all faculty members, but one's success need not be measured solely by one's publishing portfolio. 3) Teaching is described as a high institutional priority, but faculty selection, promotion, and tenure decisions tend to focus on the single measure of one's scholarly record. 4) Institutional goals state the prominent role of teaching and learning, but evidence is seldom found in annual reports to demonstrate this commitment. 5) The advancement of knowledge is a clear priority, and yet essentially the same rewards and encouragement are routinely given to trivial scholarship as are given to more substantial work. 6) Publications are more often counted than professionally evaluated. 7) Rarely is the application of one's scholarship to the classroom measured. 8) And finally, there is almost a total disregard for the time and energy devoted to teaching and how that might relate to the level of rewards given to teaching. If reform is to be successful, issues of this type must be debated and resolved.

Discarding the Sacred Shields

Every profession has its share of sacred cows; higher education is certainly no exception. While such barriers commonly appear when change seems imminent, often the sacred areas are not even broached in discussion. Obviously, the future cannot be built around these undiscussed areas. Therefore, certain perspectives must be openly debated for the future requires new solutions that reshape existing structures.

Faculty evaluation is without question the one area that is most commonly singled out as being guarded by a series of sacred shields. Evaluation deficiencies permeate the academy and visibly demonstrate the unwillingness of a sizeable portion of the professoriate even to address the topic. Some seem insulted when the question is broached and totally reject the notion. Others express a fear about developing evaluation procedures and have a mistrust in colleague and administrative use of evaluative data. Another large segment of the profession places narrow confines on how the evaluation of instruction should be conducted.

Clearly, the single most prevalent defense mechanism is that "teaching cannot be evaluated." The belief in this myth makes higher education a public laughing stock. Further, it is interesting to note that this is a common statement at many of the campuses that profess to be "teaching institutions." In truth, teaching can be assessed as rigorously as research and publication. Numerous works over the last decade by William E. Cashin, Wilbert J. McKeachie, Peter

Seldin, and countless others report how systematically collected data from a variety of sources can be used to validate teaching performance. For teaching to assume its rightful role, this sacred shield must be set aside.

The evaluation of instruction must include the full range of a faculty member's responsibility. Attention must be directed to professional competence measured in terms of content expertise, classroom preparation, organization of material, and classroom presentation. Data, insights, and input on teaching must be evidenced from a variety of sources. Only when evidence of this type is available can consideration be given to the construction of appropriate reward structures.

In addition, there is a need for better dissemination of information about the evaluation of instruction. Instruments and data systems need to be improved, and the concepts underlying the evaluation of instruction need to be understood by all segments of the profession. Professional development programs need to be established so faculty can better understand the basic methods of evaluation. These demands for change are substantial and extend far beyond what might be seen as simple refinement; since they have not been resolved, they have placed the profession in a defensive position. The professoriate must respond positively to reassert the importance of teaching. It must seize the current opportunity to demonstrate the inherent quality of the academy.

These demands for change are substantial and extend far beyond what might be seen as simple refinement; since they have not been resolved, they have placed the profession in a defensive position.

While much of the discussion thus far has focused on evaluating teaching, the effective evaluation of scholarship cannot be overlooked. While instructional variations will result from individual missions and priorities, the profession cannot accept an "either/or" posture of focusing on teaching or scholarship. The integral nature of the two must be firmly intertwined. Ernest L. Boyer vividly illustrates this point:

> *[H]ere an important distinction should be drawn. While not all professors are or should be publishing researchers, they, none-theless, should be first-rate scholars. We understand this to mean staying abreast of the profession, knowing the literature in one's*

field, and skillfully communicating such information to students. To weaken faculty commitment to scholarship, as we define it here, is to undermine the undergraduate experience, regardless of the academic setting.

Further, the results of such scholarship should be made available for judgment. There are many ways to do this: Apart from publishing books, monographs, or articles in journals, a scholar can write textbooks, participate in conferences, develop new approaches to instruction, and most especially, be more effective in the classroom. In one or a combination of these ways, such activities should be evaluated by peers. How else can we judge whether a faculty member is staying professionally alive?

This is the point: Scholarship is not an esoteric appendage; it is at the heart of what the profession is all about. All faculty, throughout their careers, should, themselves, remain students. As scholars, they must continue to learn and be seriously and continuously engaged in the expanding intellectual world. (3:131)

Many faculty members have forgotten the importance of scholarship and practicing their own art. The complex scholarly process deserves more than a counting of the number of presentations, publications, grants, and awards. The absence of sound evaluative approaches leaves college teaching at the mercy of those who continue to promote the dichotomy between teaching and research. Simply put, if the profession does not effectively evaluate the totality of teaching and devise alternative modes to assess all aspects of scholarship, the professoriate will abdicate an important professional responsibility.

Simply put, if the profession does not effectively evaluate the totality of teaching and devise alternative modes to assess all aspects of scholarship, the professoriate will abdicate an important professional responsibility.

A final set of shields surround the classroom. While the sanctity of the classroom is and should be a valued tradition, like so many virtues, when carried too far, it can become a negative. Concealed under the protective shield of academic freedom, the evaluation of instruction has been ruled off limits by some. It is as if there is some inalienable right to be incompetent or at least not to be required to prove competence. In some cases, the protectionism philosophy has carried over to the evaluation of teaching -- "everyone is an outstanding teacher."

While the sanctity of the classroom is and should be a valued tradition, like so many virtues, when carried too far, it can become a negative.

A realistic appraisal of each discipline demonstrates the point that only through the evaluation of classroom activity can one fully assess the scholarly competence of an individual. The complexity of knowledge renders it impossible to validate one's competence in a discipline through the authorship of one or two articles. Daily teaching contacts, however, provide countless opportunities for faculty members to demonstrate their scholarship -- the introduction of new insights/research can be tested, the development of new materials can be evaluated, the relevancy of curriculum initiatives can be assessed, and the appropriateness of content can be measured. Simultaneously, the actual preparation, organization, and presentation skills of teaching can be judged.

Regardless of the reason, the profession must willingly acknowledge these problems and take steps to correct the situation. Higher education cannot be a static operation. The demands placed on the academy are different today as the needs of society have become more diverse. The decades ahead will place even greater expectations on its professionals. It seems ironic that many academics who have accepted the professional challenge to pursue the unknown, to discover new knowledge, and to stimulate change within their own disciplines have such great difficulty in accepting these tenets for themselves and their own teaching. Difficult as it may be, these demands must be addressed, and the governance structures of higher education must respond. Steps must be taken and support mechanisms introduced that move faculty members toward the goal of reaching their highest potential.

It seems ironic that many academics who have accepted the professional challenge to pursue the unknown, to discover new knowledge, and to stimulate change within their own disciplines have such great difficulty in accepting these tenets for themselves and their own teaching.

Creating a New Agenda

These myths, issues, and sacred cows reveal some of the undercurrents present in the academy. It takes little effort to acknowledge that existing structures do not present a workable framework for the future. The lack of credible models for evaluating faculty members is not acceptable. Equating the value of research with the number of publications is an embarrassment. The lack of scholarly substance and the sole pursuit of long bibliographical lists is demeaning to the profession. And, the unwillingness to evaluate the full range of the teaching/learning process is a serious indictment of the profession. Faculty members who are teacher scholars are needed. They need to be properly equipped with effective teaching competencies and have a thorough knowledge of their disciplines. Most importantly, they must be evaluated on their ability to demonstrate these competencies.

Faculty members who are teacher scholars are needed. They need to be properly equipped with effective teaching competencies and have a thorough knowledge of their disciplines. Most importantly, they must be evaluated on their ability to demonstrate these competencies.

To many, what has been said may sound radical. To some, the pointedness of the comments may seem reactionary. However, the tensions and issues raised are real. Whether controversial or not, these perspectives do reflect much of the transitional period in which higher education is immersed. While these issues are imminent, changing the culture of academia will not be an easy task. As recently suggested by the Pew Higher Education Research Program:

> *[P]erhaps more than any of the learned professions, the professionals themselves define the culture they inhabit. The academic freedom of faculty has protected them not just from external interference, but from internal controls; they take orders from no one, least of all their peers and colleagues. They prize their independence, their ability to define for themselves how best to teach and the kinds of scholarship they wish to pursue. (11:4)*

The responsibility of institutional leaders is to accept this challenge. They must exert pressure on the internal structures of the academy. Faculty members need to make the same demands for good teaching as they do for quality scholarship.

The academy must affirm the role of the teaching scholar. Priority statements supporting teaching are needed. The artificial dichotomy between scholarly activity and teaching must be dismantled. Means are needed to demonstrate how scholarship bolsters teaching and teaching fosters scholarship. The connections between teaching, learning, content, and scholarship need to be defined. Evaluative procedures need to translate these relationships into actions that produce specific, measurable forms of evidence. Bold steps must be taken to move the academy back in touch with the professional responsibilities of the faculty and the educational needs of the students.

Bold steps must be taken to move the academy back in touch with the professional responsibilities of the faculty and the educational needs of the students.

Alternatives

Premise

Change depends upon new alternatives being presented.

Challenge

To lead a change process, one must:
- Establish new philosophical frameworks
- Develop new workable alternatives
- Create new environmental orientations

CHAPTER 3

BUILDING A NEW FRAMEWORK

The challenge of any change-oriented initiative is to ensure that it is based upon sound principles. As simple as this task may seem, change agents are often confronted with a series of operational problems that compound the task. How will the change be implemented? What new procedures will be needed? What strategies will be used to communicate the plan? Will the change create other problems? The list of questions is, of course, formidable. The extent to which such factors are allowed to detract from the development of a sound philosophical position only tends to lessen its chances of success. Careful attention must be given to building a new framework before implementation efforts are undertaken. This challenge provides the fundamental purpose of this chapter.

Leaders must be willing to ask: What are the purposes of faculty scholarship? Is scholarship valued differently by the institution than its faculty? What are the relationships between teaching and scholarship? How does scholarship ensure content competencies in the classroom? How can faculty members demonstrate that they are current and up-to-date? While some may express doubt that the academy will examine these issues, the fact remains that faculty members are uniquely prepared to conduct analyses of this type. There is no reason to believe that Ph.D.'s who routinely analyze complex philosophical issues or technical problems in their disciplines are somehow incapable of the same analysis of the fundamental values of higher education.

Clearly, higher education is steeped in tradition much of which is integral to its basic nature. The critics may be right when they suggest that little change will likely occur in the rewards and recognition structures of teaching during the nineties. However, five years ago little change was projected in the economic structure of Europe and practically nothing which has recently come to pass in

Eastern Europe and the Soviet Union was anticipated. The very nature of the challenge of attempting to determine the proper balance between teaching and scholarship will raise conflict. Strong positions will be taken on both extremes, but the dialogue must commence.

There is no reason to believe that Ph.D.'s who routinely analyze complex philosophical issues or technical problems in their disciplines are somehow incapable of the same analysis of the fundamental values of higher education.

For some, the debate will signal the demise of the academy as we know it. While this point will likely be well articulated, it is difficult to imagine such a demise. For others, the interchange will shed new light on topics rarely discussed. On this extreme, unfortunately, sizeable numbers of the professoriate have given little attention to why scholarship is important beyond, of course, its tangible impact on tenure, promotion, and merit. Still others will profess that the current system is working fine and is not in need of reform. Somewhere between these extremes, we must generate a new point of reference. A new middle ground must be established!

To accomplish this task, this chapter is organized under three major headings--reasons for faculty scholarship, purposes of scholarship, and implications of the teacher scholar continuum. This final section provides detailed illustrations of how the profession can move toward a teacher scholar framework.

Somewhere between these extremes, we must generate a new point of reference. A new middle ground must be established!

Reasons for Faculty Scholarship

To build a new framework requires more than superficial responses based on perceptions or personal values. Often, what is assumed as a basic belief may not be as commonly accepted as perceived. For example, most faculty will likely respond that they have a clear understanding of why faculty scholarship is important. "One needs to demonstrate that he/she is current!" "It is a way to keep up-to-date." "It's important in the promotion and tenure processes." "The University requires it!" "I enjoy it; it gives me great satisfaction!"

As one begins to analyze such statements, it soon becomes clear that there are more substantial reasons why faculty members are involved in scholarship. Similarly, there are reasons why individuals at certain institutions convey different views. Even within a department or college, there may be widely diverse views expressed among colleagues. In some cases, this variance of opinion is, in fact, an institutional strength. But if these individuals are asked to meet the same standards or tests for promotion, or to present the same amount of scholarship for tenure, the alliance breaks down. In the same regard, institutional priorities need not necessarily determine the outcome of the evaluation of an individual faculty member's scholarship. Without the development of clearly articulated statements, a faculty member's tenure status may depend more upon one's perceived status in the institution than upon one's actual competence.

To place this dilemma in perspective, major research universities are commonly criticized for sending away bright young teachers because of inadequacies in their records of research and scholarly activity. Administrators are regularly criticized for paying lip service to teaching excellence and then promoting individuals because of distinctive research records and prolific publication lists. While the merits of individual cases may vary, the common perception is that research productivity regularly wins out over teaching. What has really happened in most of these situations is that individuals in the institution have not clearly articulated their own values. Typically, when a new faculty member is terminated for lack of scholarly activity, the system has failed. Such faculty members have not been properly guided by their colleagues. The role of scholarship has not been effectively communicated. The new member has not properly assumed his/her professional responsibilities. Administrators have not demonstrated the distinction between the classroom performance on a short-term basis and the need to demonstrate professional disciplinary competence over an extended career. Similarly, the system has failed when the weak classroom instructor with a strong scholarly record is tenured or promoted. Again, deficiencies can be noted for all parties, and at all levels, but the major flaw rests with the departmental members who failed to evaluate their colleagues' teaching qualifications. Regardless of the perspective, the professoriate needs to understand and clearly delineate the differences between institutional and individual faculty perspectives. These differences need to be carefully stated and then translated into operational terms in the various reward and recognition structures of the institution.

Without the development of clearly articulated statements, a faculty member's tenure status may depend more upon one's perceived status in the institution than upon one's actual competence.

Institutional Perspectives

The research capacity of American higher education is an international success story. Actions taken by the federal government over the last fifty years along with corresponding campus-based initiatives have fostered the establishment of a sophisticated research component in the academy. There is no question that these actions have propelled higher education well beyond what might have been the expectations of President Franklin Delano Roosevelt.(2) While gains have been made, most faculty would also agree that the resulting publish or perish syndrome is out of balance. Clearly, part of this problem rests with the profession and its inability to separate institutional perspectives from individual interests. The first step in achieving a better balance is to understand both.

There are several reasons why an institution might encourage the development of research, grants, and other forms of creative and scholarly activity. Generally, such interests might be grouped under one or some combination of the following:

- Academic Accomplishment
- Competitive Advantage
- Evaluative Ranking
- Financial Gain
- Prestige

Each of these reasons provides sound rationale for institutional investments that support external grant and internal research activity. The fundamental issue that must be resolved, however, rests on the need to limit the amount of undue institutional influence over the academic rewards structure. Naturally, the higher level of importance given to research by an institution, the greater the amount of attention placed on the traditional measures of scholarship. It is imperative, however, that the importance of instructional priorities be maintained. The research initiatives of the institution should not be allowed to get out of balance with the instructional goals of the faculty. Measures that are used to evaluate institutional effectiveness must be separated from faculty reward structures. Campus decision makers must learn to construct appropriate means of recognition that respond to institutional priorities. Such efforts must be conceived within a framework that appropriately balances a faculty member's commitment to content competence (classroom based) and scholarly accomplishment (research based). Each institution **must** determine the appropriate balance between these tensions.

The research initiatives of the institution should not be allowed to get out of balance with the instructional goals of the faculty. Measures that are used to evaluate institutional effectiveness must be separated from faculty reward structures.

Individual Perspectives

As the research establishment of the academy has grown in prestige and significance, there has been a paralleling compulsion for faculty members to devote more time and energy to their personal scholarship. The concern over the publish or perish agenda has continued to grow, but little concerted effort has been made to reduce or minimize the potential conflicts induced by these forces. In most cases, the topic of separating the ways in which institutional priorities are measured from the interests of the faculty has not been broached.

For faculty scholarship to become a more integral evaluative component it must become more closely aligned with the instructional process. The connections between scholarship and the reasons why most faculty members are involved in such activities must become more pronounced. Typically, the reasons for faculty scholarship may be found in one or more of the following areas:

- Achieve Recognition/Rewards
- Contribute to Instructional Objectives
- Gain Personal Satisfaction/Accomplishment
- Impact Knowledge Base
- Maintain/Demonstrate Competence

All of these reasons provide a strong rationale for faculty scholarship to form a substantive base in any professional competence evaluation model. Approaches designed to measure these factors need to be constructed within the context of an institution's mission and focused on the relationship between instruction and scholarship. There is little room in promotion deliberations, for example, for juried articles that have little or no relationship to one's professional responsibilities. Reward structures that ignore a faculty member's currency in the content area cannot be accepted. Faculty members who are not actively involved in "practicing their art" in terms of scholarship do not have a role in higher education. For the typical faculty member, the primary role of scholarship must be to enhance and facilitate the instructional process. It seems only reasonable that if one devotes 75 to 80 percent of his/her time to activities associated with instruction that a significant portion of one's scholarship should contribute to this assignment. Anything less than insisting on current "content" competence in the classroom would certainly not fit within an acceptable accountability model.

It seems only reasonable that if one devotes 75 to 80 percent of his/her time to activities associated with instruction that a significant portion of one's scholarship should contribute to this assignment.

Purposes of Scholarship

The reasons for scholarship, both institutional and individual, provide a workable context for the development of a new conceptual framework. The issues raised by these varying perspectives only begin to suggest the extent to which careful attention must be given to all aspects of the meaning of scholarship. Surprisingly, little descriptive or analytic research has been conducted on this topic. The recent work of Ernest L. Boyer (2), as presented in **Scholarship Reconsidered: Priorities of the Professoriate**, provides an important departure in an attempt to acknowledge and analyze various forms of scholarship.

Boyer describes the dimensions of scholarship to be composed of "four separate, yet overlapping functions." These purposes are the scholarship of discovery, integration, application, and teaching. The scholarship of discovery is grounded in the basic tenets of research as normally conceived and is rooted in the disciplined, investigative efforts that permeate the academy. The scholarship of integration underscores those efforts that make connections across disciplines, interpret findings within a large context and give meaning to the research. The third area, scholarship of application, departs somewhat from the investigative and synthesizing traditions of academic life. It calls for an application of knowledge to a particular problem which may provide the basis for new knowledge or solutions. The scholarship of teaching emphasizes the final formation. As a scholarly enterprise, teaching is portrayed as a dynamic process that combines effective pedagogical procedures and current knowledges within an engaging learning environment. While these primary thrusts of scholarship may be analyzed in a singular fashion, together they form an interdependent framework for creative and scholarly activity.

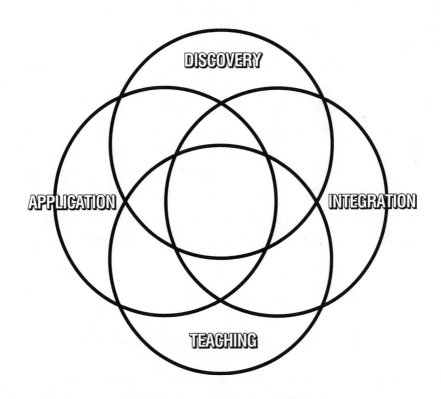

Chart 2
Functions of Scholarship

The implications of this analytic treatment of an expanded concept of scholarship are many. First and foremost, the inclusion of teaching within this structure provides a strong rationale for integrating teaching and scholarship. Potentially, this departure suggests the demise of the traditional dichotomy between teaching and research. It legitimizes the importance of conducting research on teaching. It provides credibility for the measurement of learning and other forms of student assessment. It suggests a new importance to being current in the classroom and how this relationship fits within a scholarly framework.

The delineation of these four functions also suggests many other applications for the professoriate. For example, the categorizing of scholarship provides a basis to extend beyond the typical practice of simply counting the number of scholarly works. It might be used to suggest a means to focus more directly on qualitative issues. It could be used to develop institutional, college, or departmental priorities. It could form the basis for individual plans of action. The suggested structure itself might be the source of in-depth study and research, thereby exposing some of the complexities of the concept of scholarship. Regardless of the initiatives undertaken, the four functions of scholarship provide a significantly broader view of scholarly activity. The various interrelationships present within the teaching/learning environment suggest the need to rethink what it means to be a scholar. They call into question the traditional hierarchial view that scholars conduct research, publish, and sometimes apply what they have learned or convey their knowledge to students.

The various interrelationships present within the teaching/learning environment suggest the need to rethink what it means to be a scholar. They call into question the traditional hierarchial view that scholars conduct research, publish, and sometimes apply what they have learned or convey their knowledge to students.

Integration of Teaching and Scholarship

Clearly, the time has come for some boldness in higher education. It is time to move beyond the traditional dichotomy between teaching and research. It is time to eliminate the publish or perish syndrome and replace the research scholar concept with a teacher scholar model. The debate and dialogue over the last twenty years has brought the profession to a new apex of thinking. What happens in the 1990's will likely shape actions in the initial twenty-five years of the next century. Teaching and scholarship must be integrated in principle and practice!

What happens in the 1990's will likely shape actions in the initial twenty-five years of the next century. Teaching and scholarship must be integrated in principle and practice! ... The accountability demands of our society preclude the luxury of an either/or environment.

Over the years, the academy has functioned, for the most part, as if teaching and research were separate entities. Typical comments often heard were: "If you are publishing that many articles, you certainly couldn't be doing a good job in the classroom." "My teaching is so consuming that I don't have time for research." Or, "All of the rewards emphasize publishing; besides, you can't evaluate teaching." The accountability demands of our society preclude the luxury of an "either/or" environment. One must be current in the appropriate content/scholarship area and up-to-date on current teaching pedagogy/strategies. This is a demanding situation, but the professoriate can accept no less.

The movement to integrate teaching and scholarship is not directed toward lessening the importance of scholarship. Rather, it is an effort to redefine how we describe and measure scholarship. It is seen as a means to upgrade the importance of teaching. It is designed to place greater emphasis on the relationships between teaching and scholarship. At its ultimate stage, it is an effort to determine the proper balance between the two extreme points of a continuum. It is expected that a teacher scholar will be able to explore the frontiers of knowledge, integrate ideas into instructional patterns, connect thought with action and application, and create self and student environments that facilitate learning. As suggested in Chart 3, the teacher scholar model places emphasis on professional competence that draws from the roles of a teacher and a scholar.

It is expected that a teacher scholar will be able to explore the frontiers of knowledge, integrate ideas into instructional patterns, connect thought with action and application, and create self and student environments that facilitate learning.

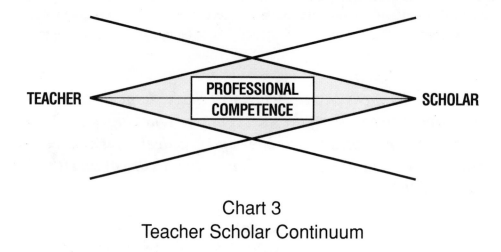

Chart 3
Teacher Scholar Continuum

Implications of the Teacher Scholar Continuum

The call to create a better balance between teaching and scholarship strikes directly at the heart of the publish or perish debate. It demands that the professoriate assess the manner in which it demonstrates its basic values. This challenge is not new, but it can no longer be ignored! It is critical that the professoriate address such basic questions as:

- What measures are needed to evaluate effectively the faculty's classroom content and pedagogical competence?

- With respect to the instructional mission of the campus, what should be the appropriate faculty recognition and reward structures?

- What alternative measures are needed to validate properly a faculty member's professional competence along the teacher scholar continuum?

- What is the proper balance between the alternative validation measures and the traditional measures as represented by national publications, presentations, and grant activity?

- What changes need to occur on campus to modify or adjust tenure and promotion procedures to accommodate this new orientation?

Overwhelming as these questions may be, it is apparent that academic leaders must apply the same standards of accountability to faculty evaluation and rewards structures as they do when raising questions about the appropriateness of specific institutional budget expenditures. The same philosophical questions as applied to academic standards must be focused on the appropriateness of the current "research scholar" model. The same rigor demanded of student performance must be extended to faculty performance. The time has come for individuals throughout the academy to demonstrate a willingness to step back and reassess the internal structures of the academy. Simply to complain about the process or to withdraw from the debate in a complacent manner will not accomplish the overriding goals. It is time to question existing assumptions, to explore new options, and to construct new structures.

The same rigor demanded of student performance must be extended to faculty performance.... Simply to complain about the process or to withdraw from the debate in a complacent manner will not accomplish the overriding goals.

Rethink the Process

The probing of the structures of higher education must start with the basic trilogy of purposes: teaching, research, and service. There is no question of the significance of these components, but the application of these functions to the faculty reward processes is different from their application to the institutional mission. As already suggested, the difference between institutional values and faculty expectations needs to be maintained. An acceptable level of excellence in teaching and scholarship for all faculty members must be defined. The role of service needs to be more clearly articulated. Institutions need to better define the differences between various forms of service and the relative importance of such efforts.

Also, clear distinctions and definitions are needed for terms such as "reward" and "recognition." For example, it seems that the term "reward" might more appropriately be used for monetary rewards that affect one's base salary such as tenure, promotion, and merit, whereas "recognition" might be reserved for special tributes, stipends, and ceremonial activities. Questions regarding the proper role of faculty members and administrators in making such decisions may need to be delineated at the same time these discussions are underway.

Regardless of the direction of these discussions, it is clear that the integration of teaching and scholarship raises serious questions about the continued use of teaching effectiveness and scholarly activity as separate "boxes" in the documentation processes for promotion, tenure, and merit. The continued practice of attempting to force action toward the extremes of the teacher scholar continuum seems counterproductive. Attention must be focused on the connections and interrelationships that exist. The reward structure must be used to reinforce the "wholeness" of the process. The use of a professional competence continuum would more likely foster this approach than would dwelling on the traditional apartheid philosophy of the past.

The Professional Competence Model illustrated in Chart 4 suggests alternative headings that might be employed in the professional documentation process. Each of the items around the perimeter (others could certainly be added) suggests a dimension that might be used in the evaluative process. These dimensions are not mutually exclusive and when assessed in a composite fashion provide a clearer sense of one's professional competence. Furthermore, this model visually illustrates how the teacher scholar continuum integrates the various aspects of professional competence. By viewing these dimensions as forces that influence or shape professional activity, a paralleling reward structure could be developed.

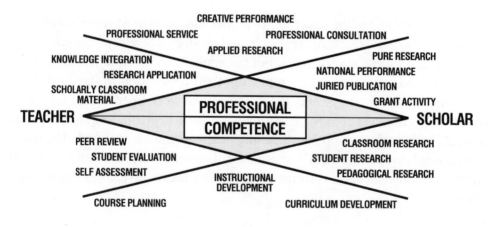

Chart 4
Professional Competence Model

A final ingredient that needs attention in the redirection effort is the development of a new set of research questions that refine and further define the Professional Competence Model. For example, over the years much has been written about research findings that demonstrate that there is not any relationship between the level of scholarship and teacher performance. Typically, these studies have attempted to compare the number of published articles and student ratings. While these studies are valuable, would one normally expect them to reveal a positive relationship? It may be possible, but for the most part such efforts are attempting to measure relationships on the extremes of the continuum. Might it be more likely that a positive relationship would exist between the level of one's scholarly activity and the extent to which one conveys current content in the classroom? It seems reasonable to expect that research directed toward this premise might be more productive. The use of the multiple dimensions in Chart 4 illustrates a vast array of research possibilities.

Broaden the Definition of Scholarship

For most of this century, the word "research" has been synonymous with excellence in higher education. Success in this area has produced a high measure of institutional prestige. Major scientific breakthroughs and inventions have been prevalent. Large research complexes have been established and large amounts of overhead income have been generated. Other than the military and a few research and development centers, the academy has had a virtual monopoly on certain types of research activity. The emergence of the information age in the last decade has in effect "deregulated" the research establishment. Computerization has produced problem solvers and research specialists throughout our society. The needs for applied research to address societal complexities has grown at a rapid rate.

The demand to broaden the intellectual base has also started to occur within the academy. The literature, as embodied in the teacher scholar movement of the last twenty years, suggests that a new set of relationships should exist. Boyer's work, as already mentioned, provides a new analytical categorization for scholarship. The increased level of attention being focused on teaching legitimizes and expands the potential research base in this area. The current societal demands for greater accountability and the spiraling costs of higher education suggest that a "re-justification process" must begin. And finally, the restlessness of the professoriate over the academy's inability to deal with the rewards structure creates yet another set of dilemmas to be faced.

The incongruencies suggested by these external and internal forces mandate reform. They suggest, too, the complexity of the agenda and counsel that change of this magnitude cannot be accomplished by a singular, short-term effort.

In this respect, there are at least four actions that deserve attention. First, and fundamentally important, is the replacement of the term "research" with that of "scholarship." To some this change may only be perceived as a subtlety, but such a change has far reaching implications. For most, the term research has a very narrow connotation. Often the application of the word research does not encompass that broad array of creative activity undertaken by scholars. It is not uncommon, for example, for faculty members in literature or the arts to insist that changes in promotion procedures include such phrases as research and creative activity. The use of the word "scholarship" would facilitate the development of a scholarship continuum that acknowledges "pure research" and "action research" as well as various forms of artistic expression and creative activity.

First, and fundamentally important, is the replacement of the term "research" with that of "scholarship."

A second area of change deals with the need for continued study of the concept of scholarship itself. The grouping of scholarship into the four interrelated functions of discovery, integration, application, and teaching provides a point of departure. The refinement of these groupings and their further delineation would allow the professoriate more readily to adapt and integrate a broadened conceptual framework. Such initiatives could also bring about a significant reordering of priorities in a third area: namely, the placement of expanded importance on all phases of the teaching/learning process. Pedagogical research must be given increased credibility so it can serve as a primary component in the teacher scholar model. It deserves an elevated status. Additionally, few faculty members have a thorough understanding of the teaching/learning process and the attendant measures of assessment. Thus, limited research is conducted on the basic teaching/learning process. It is hard to imagine a major corporation such as IBM not dedicating a major portion of its resources to research on computers. Yet, higher education only gives lip service to the importance of conducting research on the basic teaching/learning processes. Attention must be given to this issue. The relationships that exist in the instructional process between teacher and learner and methodology and content must become a common topic of discourse.

Limited research is conducted on the basic teaching/learning process. It is hard to imagine a major corporation such as IBM not dedicating a major portion of its resources to research on computers.

The final area of change needed in the broadening of scholarship is to explore the interface between scholarship and content expertise. The academy has generally adopted a philosophy that if faculty members are productive scholars (as measured by the number of national presentations, publications, and grant activity), they are competent in the classroom in terms of the content being offered. Of course, this line of reasoning has numerous pitfalls--e.g., the scholarship may be in an area outside the teaching assignment, the research may be narrow or focused in an incidental area, or the scholarly activity may not be integrated into the course materials. Steps must be taken to ensure that the natural connections between scholarship and content are in place and analyzed. Alternative means of validating that one is current in the field need to be developed. Provision needs to be made so the various forms of scholarship can be pursued in all disciplines and, finally, these purposes need to be clearly articulated in the rewards structure.

Steps must be taken to ensure that the natural connections between scholarship and content are in place and analyzed. Alternative means of validating that one is current in the field need to be developed.

Expand the Evaluation Base of Teaching

As already suggested, the weak evaluative bases for determining effective teaching have served as a serious detriment to the development of a teacher scholar model. Within the context of a complex world that has the ability to launch shuttle missions or deploy troops halfway around the world, it is hard to imagine that we cannot evaluate teaching. The perceived external view is that the academy is out of touch with reality; it is inept in conducting its business; it doesn't place much importance on teaching. This general attitude has also been a primary source in propelling the publish or perish syndrome to its present state of imbalance. The absence of validating teaching measures has directly led to heavy reliance on traditionally defined research. It's easy to count the published entries in the promotion dossier and announce that "teaching doesn't count around here!"

In some regards, the professoriate has been its own worst enemy in the inflation of research and the devaluation of teaching. The driving scientific force, critically important in most endeavors, has led to an over quantification of the

Within the context of a complex world that has the ability to launch shuttle missions or deploy troops halfway around the world, it is hard to imagine that we cannot evaluate teaching. The perceived external view is that the academy is out of touch with reality; it is inept in conducting its business; it doesn't place much importance on teaching.

teaching process. Often, the emphasis in the evaluative process seems to be more focused on producing valid data rather than producing information that is needed. All too often the material included in a faculty evaluation profile is limited and narrow in scope, thus providing the potential to either short-change the amount of attention given to teaching or to over-rely on data on a particular aspect of the teaching/learning process. The profile needs to include more than hearsay or anecdotal comments about one's performance in the classroom. The actual events that occur between the student and faculty member provide only a segment of the information needed to portray a complete faculty evaluation profile. Evidence that documents effective planning is needed. Other materials that fully convey the level and type of content organization are necessary. Sample instructional materials and learning strategies might be used to illustrate effectiveness. Data that analyzes the actual events that occur in the classroom are needed. The recent work of Peter Seldin (13) in **The Teaching Portfolio** further develops this concept by detailing how an information base on teaching can be created and then used for making personnel decisions and improving teaching performance. The tangible examples provided by Seldin suggest varying approaches that might be used by individuals in widely differing disciplines. Evaluations need to be provided as to one's content expertise and how scholarship contributes to an appropriate level of current content. And finally, various approaches are needed to demonstrate that actual learning has occurred. Each of these areas serves to emphasize the need for a broad-based profile that provides a total assessment of the teaching/learning process.

All too often the material included in a faculty evaluation profile is limited and narrow in scope, thus providing the potential to either short-change the amount of attention given to teaching or to over-rely on data on a particular aspect of the teaching/learning process.

To convey adequately one's level of instructional effectiveness, a broad array of information needs to be drawn from multiple sources. Again, heavy reliance on a particular source or the omission of another only tends to weaken the confidence level of the presented material. The peer review process is critical to the overall validity of any faculty evaluation profile. Materials need to be analytical and evaluative in nature. Likewise, colleague and administrative reviews must assume a clear evaluative purpose. Self-assessment information may be helpful in providing greater clarity and focus. Student evaluations are essential if the perception of the learner is to be effectively considered. Outside peer reviews might be used to provide unbiased insights as to one's application of scholarship and the applications of current thought in one's instructional materials. All of these segments need to be supplemented by a variety of different outcomes assessment data. For example, data might be drawn from individually constructed value-added instruments or national standardized examinations. Various performance measures might be used. Campus-based data from multiple sections might be analyzed. While employer and graduate follow-up surveys are often more departmentally based, they, too, may be used to provide additional insights. Only through the collection of data from a wide variety of sources can one have full confidence in the meaning of the information.

Again, the final task in expanding the evaluation base of teaching is to develop policies and procedures that **require** evaluative information on all aspects of the teaching/learning process; that **mandate** the collection of data from a variety of different sources; that **ensure** that all evaluative materials are collected and organized in a systematic fashion; and **insist** that consultative insights are provided to improve the instructional process. Steps must be taken to weave the importance of teaching into the fabric of higher education.

Translate Mission Into Action

As efforts are undertaken to implement the concepts inherent in a teacher scholar model, the individual adaptations particular to a campus must be given careful consideration. The deficiencies as evidenced in the current "research scholar model" must serve as a constant reminder of directions that should not be pursued. The mission and purposes of an institution needs to shape campus action. It is easy to see that many institutions may adopt the same definitions, but the applications made to the reward structure might vary dramatically. For example, faculty members at Ohio University and Southeast Missouri State University might accept the same definitions of scholarship and even agree on a grouping of measures as illustrated in Chart 4. They may also agree that every member of the faculty present a series of items that document effectiveness as a teacher and a scholar. At this point, however, the similarities may cease to exist. The types and amounts of evidence may vary widely. Each institution may place emphasis on widely divergent areas of the teacher scholar continuum in a manner consistent with its overall mission. At the same time, some units within these two institutions may again have several areas of common agreement. Thus, the expectations of faculty members in teacher education at the two institutions may be quite similar while those of the chemistry faculty might be dramatically different.

Regardless of the mission orientation, the teacher scholar model introduces at least five principles that directly affect the reward structure. First, the teacher scholar model places an expectation on all faculty that they are up-to-date on current pedagogy in the field and are effective in the classroom. **The reward structures must include this consideration.** Second, the teacher scholar model places emphasis on the various relationships between teaching and learning, scholarship and content, content and learning, and teaching and scholarship. **The reward structure must include this consideration.** Third, the teacher scholar model places increased attention on how a faculty member maintains professional competence. **The reward structure must include this consideration.** Fourth, the teacher scholar model places new emphasis on how one validates current content expertise and how scholarly activity is applied in the classroom. **The reward structure must include this consideration.** Fifth, the teacher scholar model places a new focus on the development of alternative measures that show a faculty member is current, up-to-date, and effective in the classroom. Again, **the reward structure must include this consideration.**

As these principles are introduced and the attendant questions are raised, the institution and its various sub-components must determine the amount of attention given to each factor in the reward structure. Throughout this process, continued reliance for guidance must be placed on the institutional mission. The appropriate level of professional activity in the various segments of the teacher scholar continuum must be determined campus by campus. Ultimately, a determination must be made as to what is the proper balance between teaching and scholarship and what are the appropriate measures to demonstrate such effectiveness.

Steps must be taken to weave the importance of teaching into the fabric of higher education. . . . Ultimately, a determination must be made as to what is the proper balance between teaching and scholarship and what are the appropriate measures to demonstrate such effectiveness.

CHAPTER 4

DEVELOPING A TEACHER SCHOLAR MODEL

While considerable attention has been focused on the unrealistic separation of teaching and scholarship, only limited efforts have been undertaken to develop an operational model. The literature forms an impressive knowledge base, but again the practical application has been missing. The group of national proponents of a teacher scholar model represent some of the foremost thinkers in higher education. Yet, their theoretical approaches have not been translated into action. Consequently, movement on the typical campus setting has been almost non-existent. Certainly the recent action by President Donald Kennedy at Stanford University is not typical. He emphasized the need to find ways to improve teaching by placing more emphasis on the resonance between teaching and research and to connect the evaluation of the two in the rewards structure. He stressed that institutions must:

> *"[C]ontrive a convergence of the strength of our research venture with the teaching of our undergraduates," [and] fully recognize the correlation between research activity and teaching effectiveness; the challenge, I believe, is to find more productive routes of interaction between these two activities.... We need an extended institutional dialogue about this challenge, because in my judgment it is at the very heart of both the problem **and** the solution.(8:2-3)*

Efforts of this type are fundamental to the emergence of a campus-based teacher scholar model. This chapter builds upon these needs and presents a tangible model that "connects what faculty members actual do" with the assessment process. It integrates teaching, learning, content, and scholarship into a comprehensive framework. In the final section, a set of qualitative measures are added to complete the model.

Roots of Reform

The reasons for the slow transition in the acceptance of a teacher scholar model are many and well documented. As suggested in earlier chapters, the unwillingness to change, the inability to introduce effective evaluation plans, and the narrowness of purpose and scope of scholarship have all contributed to the lack of movement. Similarly, faculty members have generally been lethargic in their efforts to press forward on this agenda. Many have found it easier to fall into a complacent mode and simply complain about the publish or perish syndrome or lament that the administration would never accept the change! Still other members of the academy have never fully analyzed the interrelated nature of teaching and scholarly activity. Hence, it is not uncommon for them to comment, "How much research do I need to get promoted?" Obviously, this misses the whole point--hopefully, the response they get is the same as when a student asks, "How long should the term paper be?"

Faculty members have generally been lethargic in their efforts to press forward on this agenda. Many have found it easier to fall into a complacent mode and simply complain about the publish or perish syndrome or lament that the administration would never accept the change!

On some campuses, the level of tension between teaching and scholarship has produced a real uncertainty about the practicality of doing both well or being appreciated for even trying. In interviewing faculty members and administrators at twenty leading liberal arts colleges, Nelsen found that faculty members often "put down another colleague for concentrating too much on teaching or, alternately, on scholarship." He found, however, that these tensions cannot be totally divorced from other issues.

> *Wider tensions in the profession itself may be responsible. Faculty often remarked about their perceptions of being "locked in" to a stagnant situation, their sense of being underpaid, their fear of staff reductions, the lack of enthusiasm among their colleagues. . . . Another culprit may be what can be described as the "individualization" of the professoriate. The increased specialization of graduate school training plus the growth of departmentalization within colleges and universities have led faculty to*

operate within narrow confines. . . . The tension has been heightened by increased skepticism of the quality and value of some scholarly work. The academic machine has indeed been known to produce very narrow, sometimes not very meaningful publications. . . . A related source of tension is what some faculty called a false view of professionalism. To be professional in the minds of some faculty means directing all your time and energy to your discipline, your research, and your professional association. Some ask, where are the students in all of this?

*Colleges cannot eliminate all the forces that have recently plagued the teacher-scholar. Some are economic, social, and political forces which must be dealt with at more comprehensive levels. But colleges can renew and protect the teacher-scholar in many crucial ways. They can change their reward structures, their evaluation systems, their curriculum to encourage improvement of **both** teaching and scholarship. They can, through corporate faculty activity, work against the individualization of the professoriate; they can by their words and deeds, demonstrate a broader approach to professionalism; they can provide clearer signals and expectations for faculty to encourage high-quality scholarship **and** teaching.(9:7-8)*

Fundamental to this process is the development of a teacher scholar model. The need to develop a new philosophical framework was established in Chapter 3. This chapter presents the next step; namely, the formation of a model that facilitates the implementation of the teacher scholar concept. The purpose here is to create an understanding of the various sub-components of such a model, to describe the relationship between its major components, and to suggest a means by which qualitative measures could be used to connect the model with actual rewards. In essence, this chapter presents a process of translating theory into action.

Domains of Influence

Essentially, there are four major domains of influence that may be used to characterize the essential work of faculty members. For the most part, their efforts may be grouped under content, scholarship, teaching, or learning. In describing these areas, it is recognized that there are obvious connections. Some concepts from one domain overlap another and, in some cases, embrace related assumptions. There are examples, too, that can be made where a particular individual has effectively combined various domains. Until recently, however, most authors have tended to focus primarily on one of the four identified areas.

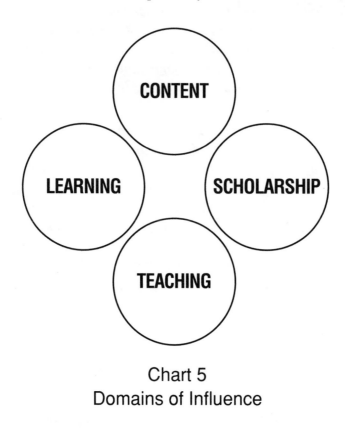

Chart 5
Domains of Influence

The **content** domain was obviously the first and initially the only area that received much attention from the profession. It formed the entire intellectual and philosophical base of what a university was all about. Faculty members were trained as content specialists. Ph.D. programs emerged as the common base to generate and validate content expertise. The Ph.D. became the singular measure of faculty excellence. For the most part, professors disseminated knowledge that was highly factual.

It was not until the coming of the Industrial Revolution that a new set of expectations was thrust upon the academy. There were demands for applied research and scientific investigation. Land grant and alternative types of institutions were formed. As the rapidity of scientific and technological change occurred, research and now more broadly conceived **scholarship** was added as an essential ingredient in the portfolio of a faculty member. While many saw the connections between content and scholarship as being most appropriate, the actual connections never extended beyond the philosophical base. Thus, little attention, even today, is given to the interrelationship that bonds the two. For example, there are no assurances in the reward structure that one's scholarship is integrated with one's disciplinary content base. There is no guarantee that one's scholarship has provided for an appropriate level of currency in the classroom. For the most part, the academy has accepted the assumption that if a Ph.D. produces a sufficient quantity of validated scholarship, the marriage between content and scholarship has been consummated.

For the most part, the academy has accepted the assumption that if a Ph.D. produces a sufficient quantity of validated scholarship, the marriage between content and scholarship has been consummated.

In comparison to content and scholarship, the area of **teaching** has been a relatively new domain. Obviously, teaching has always been an important ingredient in the educational process, and much has been written on this topic. It was not until the student protests of the 1960's that teaching emerged as major force in terms of faculty evaluation. In the teacher scholar model, however, little attention was given to the connections between teaching and the other domains. Generally, the evaluation of teaching was narrowly focused on those factors related to classroom performance. Student evaluation data served as the primary information source. In many cases peer review material was used only as a supplement. The professoriate has been slow to approach teaching from a broad-based perspective that integrates the relationships between teaching and learning, teaching and content expertise, and teaching and scholarship.

The emergence of the **learning** domain is an even more recent phenomenon. Over the years, the areas of teaching and learning have been inextricably linked, particularly in educational theory. The interdependence of the two is well researched and documented. Even so, the presence of information documenting learning in the faculty reward structures has been limited and its adaptation to the teacher scholar concept has been done only on a casual basis. On occasion, student success patterns in an introductory course have been measured on an individual faculty member basis to analyze faculty effectiveness as determined by student success in the advanced course. There are numerous other illustrations that might be made, but they do not represent the norm. Like the impact of student protests on teaching, the assessment thrust has propelled learning to the forefront. This new emphasis now provides a tangible means by which learning forms the final aspect in conceptualizing the activity of faculty members.

Relationships of Significance

The dynamic nature of the domains of influence provide a sound basis for the teacher scholar model and the reward structures that must evolve. Before attention can be given to these structures, however, the teacher scholar model must be clearly defined and the relationships between the various domains detailed. In essence, the theoretical base must be firmly established as an integrated whole, so the sub-components may be translated into an action-oriented evaluative structure.

Basic as this task may seem, the profession has not wrestled with such definitions and relationships. Clearly, however, the teaching and learning knowledge base is expanding rapidly, as K. Patricia Cross recently wrote: "Teaching is emerging as one of the most profoundly intellectually challenging aspects of our jobs as college faculty." She continues:

> *The reason teaching isn't generally treated as a highly intellectual activity is because it is practiced at such a primitive level. Professionally, it stands where medicine stood a hundred years ago. Doctors were out there doing the best they could with the knowledge available--which wasn't much. Most doctors learned their trade by apprenticeship, in which ignorance as well as experience was passed along generation after generation--much as potential college teachers learning their trade today. . . . Learning is not so much additive, with new learning simply added to the old, as it is an active, dynamic **process** in which the connections are changed and the structure reformatted. The excitement of learning comes when new connections are made, sometimes transforming the structure, pulling apart some connections and making new ones.(6:4-5)*

These same connections must be present in a teacher scholar model.

Rather than focusing on the domains of influence as independent entities, they must be conceptualized as a set of overlapping spheres, each interacting with the other, thereby influencing the whole. As illustrated in Chart 6, a multidimensional set of relationships dominate the model, blurring the actual point where one sphere begins and the other ends. To fully understand the model and appreciate the integral nature of the domains, the various relationships among each must be explored.

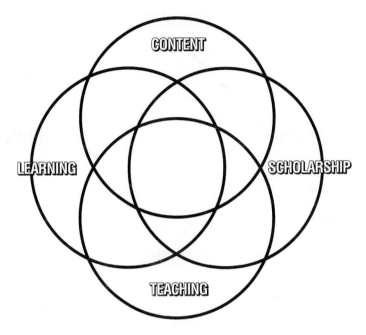

Chart 6
Interdependent Relationships

Rather than focusing on the domains of influence as independent entities, they must be conceptualized as a set of overlapping spheres, each interacting with the other, thereby influencing the whole.

Interrelated Connections

Connecting the center points of the four spheres establishes a diamond shape. Symbolically, the four corners can be used to represent the focal points of the four connecting relationships that are formed--teaching/ scholarship, content/

scholarship, learning/content, and teaching/learning (see Chart 7). In each case, the refinement of the four connecting continuums requires responses to a set of basic questions raised in this section. The results from these debates will produce variations within the teacher scholar models that are developed.

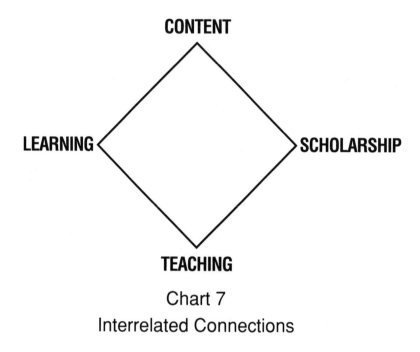

Chart 7
Interrelated Connections

Correspondingly, the specific framework developed for campus-based evaluation and reward structures will vary. Each set of conditions, however, should be grounded in the resulting responses that define the relationships existing among teaching, scholarship, content, and learning. The following examples are provided to suggest a starting point for this process.

Teaching and Scholarship. As already emphasized, the contrived dichotomy between teaching and scholarship is at the crux of the publish or perish syndrome. For decades, large segments of the professoriate have proceeded in their day-to-day actions as if these two components were separate and unrelated activities. Research has been conducted on the perceived value and importance of each, but little has been done in a practical sense to connect the two. Scholarly activity has been directed toward a particular discipline, and teaching performance in the classroom has been independently evaluated. While some research efforts have been undertaken to determine the relationship between the number of scholarly works and student evaluations, the applicability of this research has been limited.(15) As might be expected, the positive correlations between the two have, for the most part, been nonexistent. While the profession has been slow to allow teaching and scholarship to merge, there are several recent indications that the barriers are beginning to crumble. It is almost as if some mystical shroud of contamination has been removed. Numerous professional associations now have sections and programs on teaching integrated into their regular conference format. **The Teaching Professor** newsletter and discipline-oriented journals such as **Teaching Political Science, Teaching of Psychology**, and **Teaching Sociology** have gained increasing attention and respectability. The work of Ernest L. Boyer (2) has legitimized the scholarship of teaching as an acceptable scholarly activity. K. Patricia Cross (6) has demonstrated the importance of classroom research and how it can be integrated as a learning strategy and an assessment tool.

While the profession has been slow to allow teaching and scholarship to merge, there are several recent indications that the barriers are beginning to crumble. It is almost like some mystical shroud of contamination has been removed.

The adoption of the teacher scholar concept forces the integration of teaching and scholarship into a single continuum. As illustrated by Chart 4, there are numerous ways in which these two domains interrelate. While the connections between teaching and scholarship may seem clear, one cannot simply make such a statement and expect the two to be merged. The first obligation of campus leaders in trying to define these relationships is to raise a series of questions. For example, one might start by exploring the various issues associated with pedagogical research. How important is this type of research to the academic community? Does it have varying roles of importance in particular disciplines? Are certain types of pedagogical research more important than others? How should it be valued in the promotion and tenure processes? What types of qualities or measures should be present so the effectiveness of pedagogical research can be evaluated? Another approach might focus more on an analysis of the teaching process. In this regard, validation studies might occur in different disciplines across campus. Questions might be raised as to the effectiveness of particular teaching styles. Others in the same discipline might experiment with alternative approaches to integrating new knowledge into departmental offerings. Still another point of emphasis might be directed toward determining the appropriate balance between teaching and scholarship in the merit pay plan. Here, questions may be asked to more clearly define individual plans. For example, what are the scholarly expectations in presenting teaching effectiveness data? What are the expectations to publish innovative or other teaching-based forms of scholarship? What research is planned in the specific area of teaching responsibility?

Regardless of the direction of this deliberative process, the leadership cadre (faculty and administration) on campus must form some common understandings about the various relationships in the teacher/scholarship continuum. Through this process, the purpose of scholarship will be broadened, but campus leaders must ask "how far on **our** campus?" The applied nature of scholarship will be promoted, but institutional decisions must be made regarding "what levels and to what extent on **our** campus?" The teaching process will be analyzed and studied but, again, "what will be the appropriate relationships between pedagogical research and disciplinary research on **our** campus?"

The level of success in this early developmental stage is critical to applications that will be made later. The campus must come to agreement, and campus leaders must be able to express (preferably in writing) these understandings. When there is a position paper present on campus that articulates these philosophical relationships, then it is time to consider the translation of the teacher scholar model into tangible evaluative measures in the promotion, tenure, and merit reward structures.

Content and Scholarship. The scholarship domain also serves as the connecting point for the content/scholarship continuum. The relationships present in this continuum provide the fundamental reasons why faculty members attest to the importance of scholarship: namely, to stay current and extend the knowledge base. While the professoriate has long embraced these concepts, little has been done beyond a philosophical sense to ensure the connections are made. The profession has accepted, with blind faith, that if one is an active practicing scholar, one's knowledge base is current. Furthermore, if this is true, then one's content base in the classroom is current. Obviously, the premise seems logical and everyone wants it to be true! An intellectual model must do more than simply acknowledge or propose such assumptions. The teacher scholar concept must define in such a manner that connections are drawn, assurances are provided, and relationships are clarified. Again, it is the responsibility of campus leaders to insist that these issues are addressed.

Logical as the connections between content and scholarship may seem, it should not be assumed that the discussions aimed at delineating these tenets will be easy. Campus administrators must be ready to hear the onslaught of cries depicting the infringement of academic freedom. Also, faculty colleagues will

The profession has accepted, with blind faith, that if one is an active practicing scholar, one's knowledge base is current. Furthermore, if this is true, then one's content base in the classroom is current.

likely raise issues about the sanctity of the classroom. The expression of such fears, however, misses the point. Clearly, these valued traditions must be protected, but the academy must also expect a high degree of professional expertise from every member. Steps must be taken to ensure that faculty members are current and the content taught in classes is up-to-date. No professional has the right to be incompetent or to present out-of-date material!

The questions to be raised, then, focus on defining and articulating the expected relationships between content and scholarship. Again, there are numerous approaches that might be utilized by campus leaders to elevate this discussion. To illustrate, campus leaders might focus on the importance of faculty members being current in the classroom. One could then raise such questions as: How is scholarly activity used to shape the curricular process? How does one demonstrate that current theory has been integrated into classroom content? What relationship should exist between one's scholarship and teaching specialty? How can a faculty member demonstrate that he/she is up-to-date?

No professional has the right to be incompetent or to present out-of-date material!

Another approach that might be selected is for campus leaders to address the issues through a series of questions directed toward the importance of faculty members being practicing scholars. Why is scholarship important? What should be the role of scholarship in determining one's content competence? Should research that is unrelated to one's disciplinary area have the same value as that which is in one's area of program responsibility? How could the institutional mission statement be worded to properly reflect the extent to which the institution values the relationships between content and scholarship?

Individual faculty members may want to avoid discussions centered on these issues and move quickly to what's foremost on their minds--"determining what really counts around here to get promoted!" Premature movement to these very real questions may not be in the best interest of the campus. The "value" statements about the relationships between content and scholarship are essential guides in formulating the evaluative measures that operationalize these basic principles. Theory must guide process. Discussion must precede action.

Learning and Content. The pursuit of knowledge is the lifeline of intellectual activity. As the first and singularly most important function, for decades the content domain dominated almost all of the early practices of the academy. Subject matter dominated all thought. As universities grew, students were often held in disdain. ("If they don't learn, it's not my fault.") Professors were fashionably late for class. The scholar, and later the research scholar, were at the pinnacle of the academy. And, as a natural extension, the research emphasis became a logical manifestation of this influence. Learning, on the other hand, has had quite a different form of development. In the early years, it was as if learning was somehow reserved for a very few. Master teachers served as mentors in an apprenticeship-like system. Although some great teachers are still remembered for their concern for learning and the development of their students, much of this influence was lost over the last one hundred years as American higher education tried to respond to the concept of mass higher education. It was not until the student protests of the 1960's that learning began to emerge as an important area of influence. This emergence was coupled with major developments in the fields encompassing learning theory. While learning theory had long been a growing field of intellectual activity, somehow its application to higher education has been ignored. Only with the recent advent of the assessment movement has learning been propelled forward as a major component of a teacher scholar model.

While learning theory had long been a growing field of intellectual activity, somehow its application to higher education has been ignored.

The evolutionary roles held by knowledge and learning have left the learning/content continuum grossly underdeveloped. Such neglect cannot be allowed to continue if a comprehensive teacher scholar model is to emerge. The relationships between these two domains must be developed. The issues involved in exploring the relationships between learning and content are not unlike some of the potential controversial issues that exist on the other continuums. Again, campus leaders need to maintain a clear sense of purpose as they lead these debates. This is not the time to address such issues as the impact of national testing programs, the use of value added assessments, or the content emphasis in a particular discipline. As a beginning point, campus leaders might raise such questions as: To what extent should course objectives and student learning outcomes be used? What are the appropriate means to determine what content is to be learned? How much learning can be expected? How can it be facilitated? How should it be measured? What comparisons should be drawn? If national data are available, what is the appropriate use of such information?

Because of the current emphasis on assessment, faculty tendencies to move back and forth between theoretical and practical applications may not be as potentially disruptive in this debate as would be likely in discussions about the relationships on the teaching/scholarship continuum. Still, it is important that the relationships between learning and content in the teacher scholar model be properly delineated before the evaluative measures to be used in the reward structures are finalized.

Teaching and Learning. The teaching/learning continuum is the final component at the base of the teacher scholar model. The teaching and learning domains probably complement each other more than any of the other areas. In many ways they are seen as having a hand and glove relationship. From a teacher scholar perspective, however, these relationships are greatly underdeveloped and their application to the rewards structures is virtually non-existent. A broadening of the scope and articulation of relationships between the two are fundamental to their effective integration.

For the most part, the teaching domain has been heavily dominated by the measurement of classroom performance as judged in student ratings. Evaluating teaching is a far more complex endeavor that requires multiple inputs. Relationships need to be analyzed regarding the planning, organizing, presenting, and feedback segments of the teaching/learning process. Measures from a variety of sources need to be used to provide broad-based perspectives. Similarly, the scope

---

The teaching and learning domains of influence probably complement each other more than any of the other areas. . . . These relationships are greatly underdeveloped and their application to the rewards structures is virtually non-existent.

---

of the learning domain, itself, needs further study. Current literature about learning theory needs to be analyzed. Questions need to be raised about the appropriateness of active learning, for example, to various situations in the academic setting. The assessment of learning also needs further study, and the professoriate must demonstrate a greater willingness to compare and analyze data from a variety of different sources.

As with the other continuums in the model, campus leaders need to raise numerous questions so the various relationships between teaching and learning can be fully articulated. For example, what are the relationships between particular teaching approaches and learning? How can these relationships be measured and analyzed? What type of research should be conducted? What impact on learning do alternative teaching methods have? Can the appropriateness of a pedagogical approach be determined by student learning? How can graduate follow-up assessment data be used to improve instruction?

Once the answers to questions of this type are forthcoming, the issue of developing appropriate indicators of effectiveness can be addressed. Evaluation procedures are much easier to develop once the measures of success have been fully developed. Again, the primary relationship existing between the domains must be understood before specific forms of evaluation can be constructed.

Evaluation procedures are much easier to develop once the measures of success have been fully developed.

Intellectual Interactions

The teacher scholar model focuses attention on the four domains and their various interrelationships. The perimeter formed by this diamond shape provides a basis for discussions to center on the model itself; it presents a means to describe the model; and it establishes a framework for the development of an evaluation structure that can be used in tenure, promotion, and merit considerations.

While the area within the perimeter is not essential to understanding the fundamental nature of the teacher scholar model, it cannot be ignored, for it forms the basis for all intellectual interactions inherent in the teaching/learning processes. Chart 8 illustrates this interactive nature. It is as if intellectual molecules (thoughts, ideas, concepts, etc.) were bouncing around inside a container. At this stage of development, we can only describe and try to understand these interactions. It is important to note, however, that these interactions do have a bearing on specific actions that might be taken by a particular faculty member. For

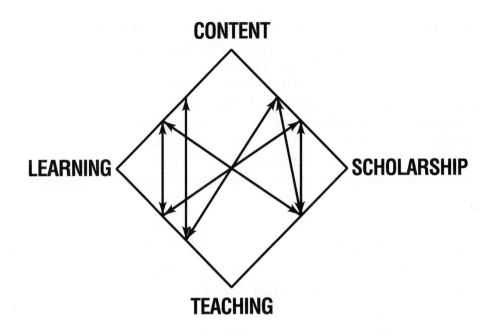

Chart 8
Intellectual Interactions

example, the content in a course may have a direct bearing on the modes of instruction that are used. The involvement of students in classroom research activities may have a direct impact on student learning. The assessment of student learning may form the basis for significant scholarly research. Similarly, certain pieces of scholarship may have a direct application on basic learning theory. Study and further development of these relationships present considerable potential, particularly in specialized areas. Campus leaders may choose to pursue these independently or incorporate discussion on these relationships into dialogue that is centered on the four primary relationships. Regardless of this outcome, individual faculty members will likely see some of these interactions as fundamental to their instructional activity. In such cases, these relationships may assume a more critical role in the teacher scholar framework.

Importance of Quality

The final component of the teacher scholar model is the addition of a qualitative dimension. The interactive nature at the base of the teacher scholar model can then be extended in a vertical direction to form a pyramid. Conceived in this manner, the theoretical model can be fully understood. Again, the "molecule concept" can be applied to illustrate the various interactions that are occurring within the pyramid model. Intellectual processes and quality are constantly interacting. The higher the forms of intellectual activity and the higher the levels of quality, the closer the interrelationship. Thus, as one progresses toward the apex of the pyramid, clarity of the domains diminishes. For example, at the base of the pyramid it may be easier to distinguish that the thrust of an activity has more of a teaching emphasis than one of scholarship. As one progresses to higher levels of quality, these distinctive characteristics are lessened and the connections between the domains become almost interchangeable.

Intellectual processes and quality are constantly interacting. The higher the forms of intellectual activity and the higher the levels of quality, the closer the interrelationship.

Beyond these relationships, it is critical that the model accommodate the various quality judgments that must be made. Descriptions of excellence must be present in any teacher scholar model. Likewise, the measures of excellence are fundamental to the evaluative reward structures that naturally flow from these relationships. The connections between expected behavior and performed behaviors must be clear. Chart 9 visually illustrates the relationships between the qualitative dimension and the assessment of each of the four domains. Further, it expands the concept of interrelatedness between the various elements of the model.

The addition of the vertical dimension thereby serves as a means to quantify the types of information/data needed in the assessment aspect of the teacher scholar model. It extends the model by defining the amount and quality of evidence that should be present. Thus, the four planes of excellence formed by the sides of the pyramid illustrate the importance of delineating the types of material (indicators) that should be present in each plane and the levels of quality that should be expected. Faculty members can then translate these concepts into an operational framework in which expected behaviors can be understood. Once accomplished, the process of delineating the amount and type of evaluative data needed for promotion or tenure has been greatly simplified.

The four axes provide a means to demonstrate visually the hierarchial nature of performance indicators for each of the planes of excellence. The task of campus leaders, then, becomes one of defining the importance (value) of the various

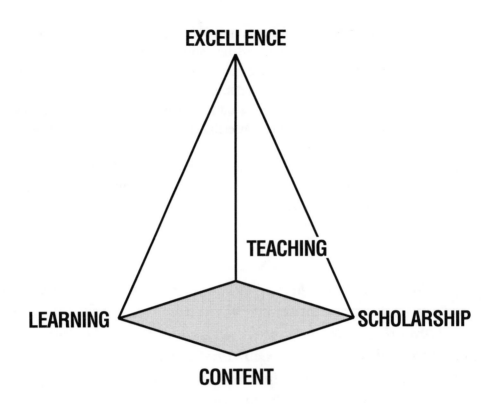

EXCELLENCE

TEACHING

LEARNING

SCHOLARSHIP

CONTENT

Chart 9
Integration of Quality and Assessment Measures

measures used to assess each plane of excellence. Such a framework can then provide a direct transition to the development of evaluative measures in the campus reward structures. The framework in Chart 9 also illustrates that the interconnected nature of the relationships between teaching and scholarship, for example, is more than a set of single line interactions. The entire surface developed by the triangular sides formed by teaching-scholarship-excellence, for example, suggests that various interactions are possible and that these interactions may be achieved with different measures of quality. The same is true, of course, with the other sides of the pyramid. Thus, a series of interrelationships are formed in which the quality of an activity is constantly interfacing with the activity itself.

The connections between expected behavior and performed behaviors must be clear. . . . Once accomplished, the process delineating the amount and type of evaluative data needed for promotion or tenure has been greatly simplified.

As with the other parts of the model, the defining of the various qualitative measures places an enormous demand on those serving in campus leadership positions. It is not easy to answer such questions as: What are the typical ways to measure scholarship as a means to demonstrate professional competence? How can various learning measures or content evaluations be used to demonstrate individual success? What factors can be used to describe effectively qualitative achievement in each of the areas? How can effectiveness in the various relationships be demonstrated? Through debate and closure on issues of this type, the teacher scholar model can be used as a framework for determining what is to be measured and how important each element is in the professional evaluation of a faculty member. Once the theoretical model is completed on a campus, focus can shift to its application in the evaluation process.

The defining of the various qualitative measures places an enormous demand on those serving in campus leadership positions. ... Through debate and closure on issues of this type, the teacher scholar model can be used as a framework for determining what is to be measured and how important each element is in the professional evaluation of a faculty member.

Applications

Premise

Change encourages those involved to rethink the process.

Challenge

To stimulate change, those involved must:
- Analyze current practices
- Suggest new applications
- Propose measurements of success

CHAPTER 5

CREATING NEW THOUGHT PATTERNS

The two preceding chapters provide an expanded context for the study and application of a teacher scholar model within the current day-to-day life of the academic community. While these alternatives make sense, one might logically ask why it is necessary to reform the integral practices of higher education in such a wholesale manner? Look at all of the successes; in many ways higher education in the United States is the envy of the world. While one might assume this reflective posture, such an attitude misses the point.

The development of new alternatives and varying perspectives is not designed to dismantle the fundamental nature of higher education that has fostered its successes. Rather, the underlying rationale for creating new thought patterns is based on the need to develop new internal structures that will allow the academy to better address the present issues and future demands. As has already been suggested, the lingering ambiguities within higher education are not new. It is clear, however, that simple internal adjustments are not going to create the type of reform necessary to elevate the importance of teaching. An extension of the current thinking focused on the encouragement of research scholars will not guide the reform effort. An escalation of faculty discontent over the discrepancy between the conflicting values of teaching and research will not alleviate this problem. The time has come to translate the rhetoric of reform into action.

The time has come to translate the rhetoric of reform into action.

In this chapter, readers are asked to rethink and reassess the "business as usual" approach so prevalent in much of higher education. A series of varying perspectives are shared, traditional approaches are challenged, and alternative means for the evaluation of faculty members are presented. Finally, a new reward structure is proposed that translates the teacher scholar model into practice.

Practicing One's Art

An initial point of departure in this process is to delineate clearly the scope of faculty activity. The instructional responsibilities of the faculty need to become the focus of activity. Faculty members must continuously study their discipline and put applications into practice. They must be practicing scholars to maintain a state of art commensurate with the title "professor." A professor must be a teacher. A teacher must be a learner constantly testing new insights on his/her peers as well as students. Teaching, then, in its broadest sense, extends to students in the classroom, to colleagues across the campus, to scholars throughout the discipline, and to professionals in the external community as well. It is through this holistic view of the educational process that the mutual goals and needs of both the students and faculty are achieved. For the faculty members of the future, the role of the teaching scholar naturally evolves. Research and other forms of scholarship complement the teaching function and vice versa.

A professor must be a teacher. A teacher must be a learner constantly testing new insights on his/her peers as well as students. Teaching, then, in its broadest sense, extends to students in the classroom, to colleagues across the campus, to scholars throughout the discipline, and to professionals in the external community as well.

Clearly, the use of scholarship as a means to maintain and measure professional competence is a requirement of the profession. Regardless of one's discipline, the option of having no scholarly activity is not a viable alternative for the present-day professional in higher education. To be a productive member of the academic community requires that each faculty member be somewhere on the teacher/scholar continuum. The essence of a faculty member is to perform intellectual activity within an educational setting--to engage in the art of inquiry, discovery, and mastery. These demands have changed little over time. The expectations for the future, however, are quite different. A reassessment of these relationships will produce an environment where professional competence is the driving force for faculty and institutional excellence.

The implications of placing the theme of "practicing one's art" at the apex of intellectual and instructional activity are immense. The interface between these concepts produces an analytical process that creates new perspectives on how faculty members view their roles and how institutions respond to these expectations. Fundamental to this process is the formulation of a new set of intellectual questions. As an example, one might ask: How does one define professional competence? What are the expectations of a faculty member in terms of competence in the domains of teaching, learning, content, and scholarship? How are the faculty expectations in each of these areas defined? How are instructional values translated into measures of excellence in promotion, tenure, or merit decision-making processes?

Regardless of one's discipline, the option of having no scholarly activity is not a viable alternative for the present-day professional in higher education. To be a productive member of the academic community requires that each faculty member be somewhere on the teacher/scholar continuum.

Varying Perspectives

One of the major strengths of American higher education is its diversity which has been acclaimed worldwide in terms of institutional function, purpose, and scope of activity. Yet, when it comes to the evaluation of faculty, this diversity seems to diminish rapidly into a "sea of similarity." There is no doubt that the expectations of a faculty member at the University of Minnesota are different from those at Central Michigan University, which are different still from those at Gettysburg College. But when it comes to translating these expectations into procedures for faculty rewards and recognition, this diversity somehow ends!

If this diversity is to be fully institutionalized, specific attention must be devoted to the individual nature of each campus. The implementation of a teacher scholar model requires a rethinking of how leaders conceptualize their campuses. It forces the development of a more clearly defined mission that specifies instructional priorities. It provides the basis for a wide variance within college structures. And, it emphasizes the individualistic nature of the faculty. This approach requires national and institutional leaders to assess the most fundamental precepts. For example, the classic triad of teaching, research, and service may properly convey the overall purposes of an institution. But this triad need not necessarily serve as the primary categories in the promotion and tenure process. How much better would it be to address a faculty member's competence in the areas of teaching and learning or scholarship and content?

The implementation of a teacher scholar model requires a rethinking of how leaders conceptualize their campuses.

Even the use of phrases such as "research institution" or "teaching institution" convey mixed signals to the general public. Does the phrase "research institution" portray an absence of a commitment to teaching? What is the role of research in a so-called teaching institution? While we may agree as educators that "we understand" the meaning of these terms, they often confuse the general public, legislators, and other prominent leaders. Can academicians afford to foster such an ambivalence within society? Do these phrases illustrate to the public one more way in which the academic community seems to be out of touch with reality? Questions of this type are fundamentally important for most institutions. Some have not clearly defined the expectations of faculty in terms of teaching, research, and service. Many have substituted service (campus committee work) for scholarship, have failed to evaluate effectively teaching, and have not articulated the interrelationships between teaching and scholarship. In fact, this scenario may be more typical of most campuses than illustrative of a few.

Many have substituted service (campus committee work) for scholarship, have failed to evaluate effectively teaching, and have not articulated the interrelationships between teaching and scholarship.

Reassessing the Role of Service

The questioning of the applicability of the classic triad of teaching, research, and service to the evaluation of faculty performance also has implications for the traditional definitions of service. The merger of teaching and scholarship leaves service as a somewhat unnatural appendage. When combined with the practical applications of the teacher scholar model which for many faculty members calls for more attention being given to teaching, learning, content, and scholarship, the typical faculty member's response is often, "How can I do more of everything?" This is a fair response that requires attention. Some things must go!

The obvious response is that the amount of time devoted to traditionally defined service activities must be reduced. As with all proposals, this proposition is not as simple as might be implied. Service is an area, however, in which several refinements are necessary. As already suggested, the institutional service function must be separated from the professional service obligations of faculty members. Areas that relate to personal interest must be totally removed from the evaluation of professional competence. While personally fulfilling, involvement in Girl Scouts, church activities, and other civic organizations does not fit within the faculty evaluative framework. Those activities which extend the professional expertise of a faculty member need to be moved into the evaluation of professional competence in the teacher/scholarship continuum (see Chart 4). Such activities serve as practical illustrations of how the definition of scholarship may be broadened and evaluative information collected on the currency of a faculty member.

The final area of reassessment deals with how institutional service (committee activity) is used to encourage faculty involvement in campus governance structures and how it is used in the faculty evaluation process. At the onset, it is critical that the importance of faculty governance be clearly articulated. The need to establish new relationships in the teacher scholar model should not be confused with some "hidden agenda" to diminish the role of the faculty in the overall operation of the institution. While some might attempt to make this case, the teacher scholar model actually extends the role of faculty by intensifying their role in the evaluative process, by providing means to broaden the definition of scholarship, and by constructing reward structures that lead to the implementation of the model. While it may be obvious, careful attention must be given to this issue so the misperceptions of a few do not overwhelm the rationality of the teacher scholar thrust.

The amount of time devoted to traditionally-defined service activities must be reduced.

There are numerous ways in which campus leaders might move forward in their attempts to delineate more clearly the role of service on campus. A position paper approach might be used to stress the importance of service and to begin the deliberative process. The faculty senate might discuss a resolution that limits faculty activity outside the department to no more than one regular standing committee assignment. The faculty in a college might agree that no more than ten percent of the evaluation for tenure and promotion may be devoted to campus service and that none may be used for merit purposes. (Since faculty members typically self report a workload of over fifty hours per week, this would produce a target of no more that five hours a week.) A department might take the position that departmental service is an expectation and that a certain level of activity is required as a threshold for consideration of promotion. Still another approach might be to delineate more specifically the evaluative character of information regarding the effectiveness of one's service. For example, consideration might be given to using only one "campus service activity" per year in the evaluative process. Or, specific criteria might be delineated to guide the evaluation of service activities. Regardless of approach, the increased level of clarity that emerges from these processes will result in a greater understanding of expectations of faculty and an enhanced development of the teacher scholar model.

Forming Assessment Strategies

The teacher scholar concept fosters an entirely new set of discussions that have broad-based implications for the evaluation of faculty performance. It provides a framework for the assessment of faculty activities. Before this debate can transpire, the discussion must move beyond the stage of simply espousing the need to understand the relationships between the various continuums. The following illustrations suggest various ways in which the assessment process may proceed.

A campus-wide effort to broaden the definition of scholarship might be used to shape a series of discussions. If it were decided, for example, to move beyond the traditional use of counting the number of publications, presentations, and grants as a measure of scholarly activity, what alternatives might be explored? As one approach, campus leaders might initiate discussions on the additional types of evidence that might be used to validate scholarly excellence. What might be the acceptable mix, discipline by discipline, between the use of traditional and alternative measures? How could applied research be defined in such a way as to demonstrate the differing value given to local, regional, or national efforts? How might classroom currency be measured?

There are various ways in which an analysis of the teacher scholar model might be used to facilitate this process. The examples that follow illustrate how each of the four continuums (teaching/scholarship, content/scholarship, learning/content, teaching/learning) might be used to facilitate this process.

Lineal Approach. The lineal approach could be used to identify the areas of assessment on one of the continuums. Through such a process, a priority order might be established or the areas in which measurement will occur could be identified. Campus leaders might even choose to merge parts of the two continuums to create the desired impact. Chart 10 suggests a possible set of applications related to teaching and research. This approach forces a new way of conceptualizing the relationships between teaching and research. It creates the basis for new thought patterns and models.

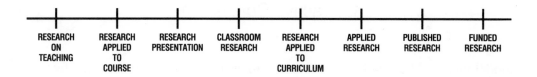

RESEARCH ON TEACHING — RESEARCH APPLIED TO COURSE — RESEARCH PRESENTATION — CLASSROOM RESEARCH — RESEARCH APPLIED TO CURRICULUM — APPLIED RESEARCH — PUBLISHED RESEARCH — FUNDED RESEARCH

Chart 10
Lineal Approach

Interactive Continuum. The interactive continuum approach serves to place greater emphasis on the interactions that may occur. As suggested in Chart 11, for example, focus is centered more on the relationships between content and scholarship. By placing emphasis on these connections, the distinctions between content and scholarship are minimized. The goal in this alternative is to demonstrate how the domains influence each other. Here, again, emphasis is placed on a new way of conceptualizing the fundamental relationships in the teacher scholar model.

Continuum Integration. The continuum integration approach builds upon the interactive nature of the teacher scholar model. In this way, the assessment measures and the importance of these measures all combine to create an assessment profile. Chart 12 illustrates the application of such an analysis to an individual faculty member. The shaded areas portray the relationship on each of the four continuums and the various assessment measures needed in the evaluation process. Once more, the use of this alternative might assist faculty members in visualizing their overall assessment profile. Further, computer

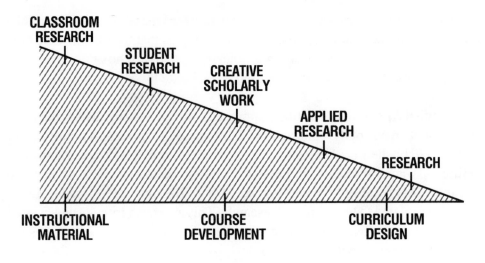

Chart 11
Interactive Continuum

modeling could be developed as a means to establish ranges of expected faculty performance in a particular department. It is time to reassess and reconsider the frameworks of the past.

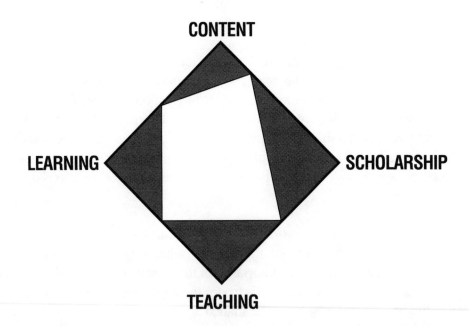

Chart 12
Faculty Assessment Profile

Evaluating Faculty Performance

New ways of approaching these issues must be found if an effective teacher scholar model is to be implemented. The adoption of a teacher scholar approach will create a "crisis need" for the evaluation of faculty performance. These requirements elicit numerous responses. In the early stages, it seems that attention should be focused on four primary areas of concern. First, clarifying the purposes of assessment and evaluation is obvious. Likewise, the importance of expanding the scope of faculty evaluation is totally consistent with the demands placed on a teacher scholar. Third, with the increases in data/information, the need to simplify the evaluative process becomes more readily apparent as does the goal to increase the amount of emphasis on qualitative evaluations. Finally, there is a critical need to translate all of these concepts into an operational set of reward structures that espouse the values of a teacher scholar. Faculty members must stand ready to receive instructional criticism to the same extent they are willing to provide intellectual criticism. They must, too, be open to questions of content competence.

Faculty members must stand ready to receive instructional criticism to the same extent they are willing to provide intellectual criticism. They must, too, be open to questions of content competence.

Clarifying the Purposes

Like all processes, it is important from the outset that the purposes of the data collection procedures be clearly stated. The narrow scope of current evaluative efforts will become more obvious as steps are taken to implement the expanded information bases as required by a teacher scholar model. This clarification process need not be complicated, but care must be taken to ensure that the proper types of data/information are collected for the intended purposes.

Essentially, there are three primary purposes for which most data are collected: 1) Self-Assessment, 2) Performance Appraisal, and 3) Institutional Recognition. Typically, self-assessment data are used for the improvement of instruction. This information is used primarily by individual faculty members for their own improvement, but it is commonly made available to colleagues in the department for other assessment and comparative purposes. Regardless of the distribution, the thrust of this information is on the improvement of instruction. Performance appraisal material is used in the typical evaluative efforts centered on promotion, tenure, and merit considerations. Considerations for these reward structures are the area requiring the greatest level of attention and are the focal point of the discussions that follow. Institutional recognition efforts sometimes draw data from these later processes, but also may require expanded information that is more specific to the award or recognition for the individuals who might be considered. Self-assessment data is always kept separated from the data used in evaluative efforts, in performance appraisal, and in institutional recognition processes used.

While the separation of processes is important, it is entirely feasible that some of the data to be used for different purposes could be collected on the same instrument. For example, a course/student evaluation might contain items related to instructional improvement and, at the same time, collect evaluative data about the effectiveness of the instruction. In this case, the separation of data would occur at the analysis phase, thereby producing two separate reports--one for self-improvement and one for performance appraisal. In this way, the sanctity of both efforts can be maintained.

Scope of Evaluation

Expanding the scope of the evaluation process is the counterpart of broadening the definition of scholarship. It expands, too, the measures used to evaluate teaching. This expansion in both the breadth and types of data/ information collected places new burdens on the academic community. It stresses the need to interface the tenets of a teacher scholar model with the evaluative process. It suggests that institutional changes must be forthcoming in the manner in which instruction is evaluated. It casts the classroom as a primary arena where the areas of faculty content and pedagogical competence are evaluated and student learning and progress are measured. The periodic review of course materials and the evaluation of how effectively these materials are used in classroom activities completes the continuous cycle of professional development and professional competence. The faculty evaluation process, thus, becomes the primary determinant of the quality of the teacher scholar. The extent to which faculty members can demonstrate that they are practicing scholars and effective participants in the teaching/learning process serves as a measure that they are deserving of the title of professor.

As already suggested, there are numerous ways in which the scope of evaluation might be expanded. Peter Seldin (13) identifies thirty different ways in which this goal may be accomplished. The examples range from descriptive materials to various products resulting from outstanding teaching. Included in the array are various evaluations from colleagues, outside reviews, peer review panels, and data from the assessment of student success.

Another illustration of how data/information could be organized might be to focus on the different aspects of the teaching/learning process. In this way, data could be grouped under such headings as Instructional Preparation, Content Organization, Classroom Performance, Student Achievement, and Follow-up Feedback. Still another approach might be to combine some of the elements in the various teacher scholar continuums. In this way, the types of evaluative categories might be expanded to include such items as:

- Content Competence
    - Application of scholarship
    - Currency of instructional materials
    - Course content relevance

- Instructional Appraisal
    - Student evaluation
    - Peer review
    - Chairperson evaluation
    - Outside consultant evaluation

- Teaching and Learning
    - Classroom research
    - Instructional experimentation
    - Value-added assessment

The expanded breadth of evaluations represented by these examples reduces the reliance on any one factor and enhances the level of confidence in instructional effectiveness by increasing the sources of input. It also diminishes the disparate effect that one indicator might have and forces individuals to review the "wholeness" of a teacher scholar.

Simplifying the Process

The academy's attempt to over-quantify data is one reason the myth persists that teaching cannot be evaluated. While much has been written on the "art of teaching," much of this theory has been discarded when it comes to the evaluative process. When the word "evaluation" is used, somehow the evaluation of teaching becomes a "science." There is little need to belabor the differences or similarities between a science or an art. There are obviously ingredients of both in the teaching/learning process. The point is, however, that in most evaluation processes in higher education, one of three decisions related to excellence should be made--is the activity excellent, pretty good, or really poor? For example, rather than trying to characterize a 3.2 on a particular item in a student evaluation form as being significantly better than a 2.8, one would only need to place it in one of these three groupings. It must be remembered that these decisions do not require the decimal precision of a honed piece of steel. Simply put, should this person be tenured or not? Should a promotion be recommended? Should a merit increase be awarded?

In the collection of data/information for such decisions, one other set of determinations must be made: namely, how important is this material. Again, this can be simplified and grouped under one of three levels of significance--primary, secondary, or unrelated. A professional judgment must be made. Similarly, an evaluation must be made of the quality of the activity. When combined, a grid can be used to group the necessary data/information needed for decision-making processes. Chart 13 illustrates a grid that is simple and easy to understand. It's adaptable to all of the major ingredients needed in the evaluation of a teacher

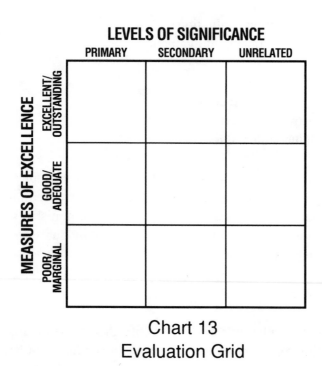

Chart 13
Evaluation Grid

scholar model. One simply needs to place each piece of evidence in one of the nine categories. When all of the evidence is combined, the final evaluative recommendation can be made.

Emphasis on Quality

The dominant trait of higher education that has prevailed throughout history is a striving for excellence. The most valued traditions of higher education are steeped in measures of quality. Whether this standard is applied to student performance as measured by GPA or graduation with honors or the competitive pursuit of research, the response has always been the same. Yet, the professoriate has been unwilling to apply the same standards of excellence to its own performance. As suggested by Boyer (3), a large proportion of faculty believe that teaching effectiveness should be the primary criterion for the promotion of faculty. Nearly half believe that at their institutions, publications are merely counted in tenure and promotion processes with no qualitative measurement. While two-thirds agreed that better ways are needed to evaluate scholarly performance of faculty, they rank publications first in the very important category for the awarding of tenure. As indicated by these perceptions, it is clear that quality is not a dominant theme in the evaluation of faculty performance.

The most valued traditions in higher education are steeped in measures of quality. . . . Yet, the professoriate has been unwilling to apply the same standards of excellence to its own performance.

Again, President Kennedy took a bold step in this direction when he recently stated to the faculty:

> *I hope we can agree that the **quantitative** use of research output as a criterion for appointment or promotion is a bankrupt idea. The over-production of routine scholarship is one of the most egregious aspects of contemporary academic life: it tends to conceal really important work by its sheer volume, it wastes time and valuable resources, and it is a major contributor to the inflation of academic library costs.*
>
> *Indeed, this issue has now come to constitute a major challenge to university science. Recent stories in national newsmagazines*

have taken up the charge that much research is without value. These allegations find some support from studies demonstrating that in many fields the majority of published papers are never cited. Many objections can be raised against the use of citation as a criterion, but it is plain that interest in this subject is high and that there is reason to be concerned about the quality of scholarly work, which surely is the important thing. The major learned societies have understood this clearly; they base election to membership on the consideration of an author's most important publications, not on his or her total production. To reverse the appalling belief that counting and weighing are the important means of evaluation, I think Stanford should limit the number of publications that can be considered in appointment or promotion. (8:9-10)

Chart 14 illustrates one way in which this challenge can be met. It combines an evaluation grid (Chart 13) with the principles embodied in the teacher scholar model. Through this very simple conceptual framework, the key concepts between teaching and scholarship, teaching and learning, content and

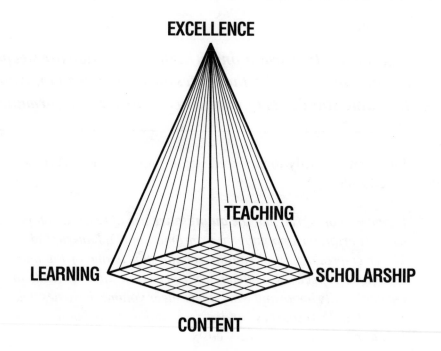

Chart 14
Performance Evaluation Model

scholarship, and content and learning are emphasized. The pyramid structure provides a visible model that represents the integration of the various continuums (e.g., triangle--Teaching-Scholarship-Excellence). Thus, the substantive areas of evaluation (represented by the base grid) are extended toward the apex of the pyramid. Quality judgments are, thus, apparent in each of the various vertical sub-components of the model.

Beyond its application to individual faculty evaluations, this model presents viable ways in which an institution, college, or department might target certain levels of acceptable performance. For example, a college may use the model to illustrate the proper balance between teaching and scholarship. Or, it might indicate the amount and performance level of learning assessment data to be provided by a faculty member. At the department level, specific performance standards might be plotted for student achievement and individual faculty members assessed within this framework.

The development of alternative evaluation measures provides specific examples of how the definition of scholarship might be broadened. They suggest tangible ways in which evaluation measures could be tied directly to the institutional mission.

Develop Evaluation Measures

Each of the four teacher scholar continuums provides a framework by which these evaluation measures may be grouped. Chart 15 illustrates that any number of cells might be created. While this example portrays a systematic grid, numerous variations are possible. One continuum might have ten cells (measures) while another could have four or five. The continuums might represent different types of measurement or efforts used to evaluate competence in a particular area. The content/scholarship continuum, for example, might include some of the traditional measures of published materials, grants, and presentations plus a series of new cells focused more on the integration of one's scholarship into classroom activity. In this case, the cells closer to the content apex might include categories on the evidence of content currency, review of instructional materials, or evaluation of course content. On the other hand, the teaching/scholarship continuum might include cells with such areas as classroom experimentation, research on teaching, pedagogical scholarship, or classroom research.

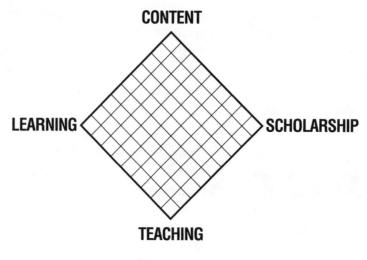

CONTENT

LEARNING

SCHOLARSHIP

TEACHING

Chart 15
Evaluation Measurement Cells

The base of the pyramid could be used to illustrate the various evaluation measures for an individual department or institution. Obviously, it is possible that an institution could identify certain common elements and departments or colleges could establish other elements. The potential options are unlimited.

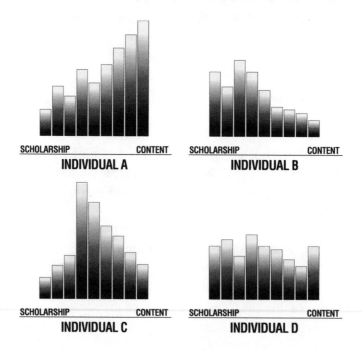

SCHOLARSHIP CONTENT
INDIVIDUAL A

SCHOLARSHIP CONTENT
INDIVIDUAL B

SCHOLARSHIP CONTENT
INDIVIDUAL C

SCHOLARSHIP CONTENT
INDIVIDUAL D

Chart 16
Variations in Evaluation

Once the type of evaluative evidence has been determined, the qualitative factor must then be added. In this way, the quality dimension can be used to demonstrate that an individual has achieved the specified level of competence. Again, Chart 16 provides four examples of what variations might be possible in the evaluation of competence in the content/scholarship continuum. The vertical quality dimension illustrates different approaches that might be considered in the evaluation of a faculty member.

Individual A, for example, is expected to produce more data and a higher level of evidence demonstrating the application of scholarship in the classroom. On the other hand, the evaluation of Individual B is centered on more traditionally defined measures of scholarship. Individual C might have a much greater focus on applied research and classroom activity. Individual D might be expected to produce a fairly consistent level of evaluative data on this continuum, but has a much greater emphasis in some other continuums. The complete faculty evaluative profile for Individual A is illustrated in Chart 17. This example portrays an individual with a substantially greater emphasis focused around teaching and learning.

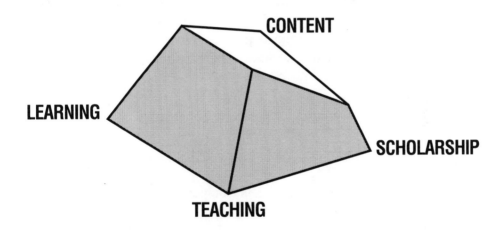

Chart 17
Faculty Evaluation Profile

The full meaning and values of being a teacher scholar can only be properly instilled in the academic community by changing existing policies and procedures. The reform must come from within through the joint efforts of faculty and administrators.

New Reward Structures

The final test in any reform effort is the actual implementation of the planned change. Fundamental to this process is the establishment of operational procedures that embody the stated concepts and principles. The teacher scholar model requires the development of new tenure and promotion procedures. While some might argue that the changes could occur with only minor adjustments, the dominance of research is so deeply ingrained that major changes are required. The full meaning and values of being a teacher scholar can only be properly instilled in the academic community by substantially changing existing policies and procedures. This reform must come from within through the joint efforts of faculty and administrators.

It seems that the profession has two primary ways in which these changes might be instituted. First, a massive revision process might be undertaken where entirely new sections of policies are developed and other sections are dropped or eliminated. Because of certain governance restraints or administrative leadership strategies, this approach might be preferred by many. Second, and probably more formidable, would be the development of new criterion. While some of the old language is reinstituted, this approach has the advantage of limiting the undue influence of current thinking. One might consider, for example, the dropping of the classic triad of teaching, research, and service. The teacher scholar model and evaluation strategies already mentioned provide a workable alternative. A new format for the organization of data/information for the promotion and tenure processes might be:

- Evidence of Teaching and Scholarship Competence

- Evidence of Content and Scholarship Competence

- Evidence of Learning and Content Competence

- Evidence of Teaching and Learning Competence

The use of these categories provides a direct link between the teacher scholar model and the evaluation of faculty performance.

The teacher scholar model requires the development of new tenure and promotion procedures. While some might argue that the changes could occur with only minor adjustments, the dominance of research is so deeply ingrained that major changes are required.

CHAPTER 6

RETHINKING THE ASSESSMENT PROCESS

In the preceding chapters, an agenda for the future was charted and alternatives to be pursued were outlined. Bringing about the change as suggested by these directions requires more than a series of proclamations. Rethinking the processes that support the academy requires more than simply exposing certain myths and sacred cows. While the new conceptual frameworks as suggested are important, faculty members must become engaged in the change process if it is to be successful. The issues raised and the proposals for change provide a new context for the dialogue that must occur.

The debate must penetrate beyond the level of structure and procedure. A clear focus needs to be centered on "what faculty do" on a daily basis and how their actions are transmitted into the evaluation process. For example, too few faculty give careful attention to the role of scholarship in their own teaching. Often there is little discussion on the importance of scholarship other than how it might relate to promotion or tenure. Few faculty members are thoroughly versed on why scholarship is important, how it relates to effective classroom performance, and what impact it has on the curriculum.

The future also demands the development of a new set of assumptions to undergird the entire faculty assessment process. Some faculty members have given thought to this challenge. They have developed specific teaching objectives, learning outcomes, and have discussed the importance of staying current. They know the importance of staying current. They well know the colleagues in their department who are practicing professionals, as well as those who are outdated. The difficulty is that this knowledge and awareness is buried under practices imposed by the publishing measuring stick. Faculty members need to develop expanded alternatives that when combined with some traditional measures demonstrate that they are current and up-to-date. The concept of "practicing one's art" needs to be further developed as a means to demonstrate the importance of being an active, involved professional. Individuals need to develop a better understanding of the teaching process and to demonstrate the connections between teaching and learning. And finally, faculty members need to demonstrate a new willingness to construct new ways of measuring success as a teacher scholar.

The debate must penetrate beyond the level of structure and procedure. A clear focus needs to be centered on "what faculty do" on a daily basis and how their actions can be transmitted into the evaluation process.

Rethinking these processes and generating discussion that ventures outside the traditional domains of thought is not an easy task. To pursue these issues, the author conducted an informal exercise with colleagues at Southeast Missouri State University. Twenty-five faculty members were asked to participate in a bit of creative thinking. The assignment they were told was simple--"The mission, should you accept this challenge, is to: 1) describe your teaching objectives and strategies, 2) indicate how you maintain professional competence, and 3) demonstrate how you validate your professional competence." Each colleague was provided with a list of questions they might address under the three areas. They were asked to organize their thoughts as seemed appropriate within a five- or six-page format.

The design of this experiment was to focus primarily on what they did as faculty members, thereby providing a different set of responses in the final section on evaluation. Demonstrating "how you would validate that you are professionally competent" was obviously aimed at the crux of the problem addressed in earlier chapters. Everything seemed easy to this point. The final set of instructions indicated that in "demonstrating ways to validate that you are professionally competent, you **cannot** make reference to published articles, presentations made, or grants that have been completed." They were told that "It is expected that every one must be practicing their art as measured by these traditional indicators. If the professoriate is to develop new applications as required by a teacher scholar model, alternative approaches and measures of effectiveness must be presented."

The months following the initial point of acceptance revealed some interesting reactions. While all of the participants were strong believers in the importance of being a teacher scholar, it was not easy for several of them to translate their beliefs into concrete statements. Four or five individuals completed the task within a month or so and demonstrated considerable comfort in proposing various alternatives. While some were busy and needed more time, others began to demonstrate an increasing level of frustration that had been caused by this assignment. Many of the faculty colleagues called on repeated occasions to gain new insights, suggestions, and clarifications. When the final results were in, three had not completed the last section and two reported only traditional measures in their effectiveness section. Two took over a year to complete the task and three others never finished. Many of the faculty colleagues commented that this was a very frustrating and difficult project to complete.

The point in sharing these insights is to emphasize that overhauling the system will not be easy. It will require concerted effort and probably a lot of group activity so individuals can constantly stimulate each other. There is, however, much that can be gained from the efforts of these individuals. It is for this reason that portions of the prepared statements are included in this chapter. Rather than using the entire text of the completed essays, sections of various manuscripts have been included under three major subheadings. The purpose of presenting these examples is to suggest the importance of connecting assessment with instructional goals; to emphasize the importance of understanding the teaching process; to demonstrate the interrelated nature of the spheres of influence--teaching, learning, content, and scholarship; and to suggest commonalities across disciplines and alternatives that might be used to validate one's professional competence.

Rethinking these processes and generating discussion that ventures outside the traditional domains of thought is not an easy task.

Describing Teaching Objectives and Strategies

A fundamental ingredient in assessing what professors do is to view their performance in terms of their instructional objectives and strategies. This starting point places specific attention and increased emphasis on the teaching/learning process. It shifts attention toward the practical side of the teacher scholar continuum, thereby providing an expanded context for the development of new evaluation strategies. To stimulate thought from this perspective, the faculty members involved in the exercise were asked to reflect on a set of questions:

- What do you try to accomplish with students?
- What are your overriding objectives?
- What particular emphasis do you bring to the classroom?
- What strategies, techniques do you use?
- What is your overall philosophy?

The examples that follow, then, present differing perspectives on how the goals of the professor can shape the assessment process. They suggest, too, that the evaluation measures and data collection procedures that evolve from this type of analysis present new applications for the criteria that might be used in promotion or tenure considerations.

A fundamental ingredient in assessing what professors do is to view their performance in terms of their instructional objectives and strategies.

Teacher/Teaching Model in Earth Science
by Ernest L. Kern, Department of Earth Science

I consider myself first and foremost a "teacher." This perception is not only consistent with my definition of the role of a university professor, but it is also consistent with what should be the primary function of the American university. Any success I may have achieved as a teacher is, in a large part, a result of emulation. Since high school I have been intrigued with "teaching" and why some individuals are "good teachers" while others are not. Through the years, I have attempted to incorporate into my own teaching of science those aspects which I have observed to be, by and large, common among successful teachers. The result is a "teacher/teaching model" that works well for me in the teaching of the earth sciences.

Central in the model is one's attitude regarding teaching: **teaching must be an individual's top priority**. Unless this is the general case (other efforts may on occasion take precedence), the other qualities that contribute to teaching effectiveness are diminished. It is our nature to work hardest at and do our best at those things we consider most important. "Attitude" is the prerequisite; it lays the background. Attitude alone certainly does not ensure teaching success; however, without the proper attitude, truly effective teaching becomes a dismally remote prospect. Against the background of "teaching as a top priority" my model includes four components which I consider vital for quality teaching.

82

The teacher must construct a positive teaching/learning affective-environment. The teaching and learning of science can be made to be lively, exciting, and fun; a look-forward-to rather than a dreaded experience. I see three subcomponents as important in the enhancement of an affective teaching/learning environment in the sciences: (a) Both teaching and learning should be in the active rather than passive mode. The class should be in a group experience, not a "one-man-show." (b) Science should be taught and learned as a hands-on, process-based experience. "Science" is a verb; one does science. A content approach (i.e., fact-filled lectures) to the teaching of science at any level undoubtedly ranks as the greatest atrocity to good science education. (c) Whenever possible, the relevancy of science to society and the students' personal lives and futures should be stressed. To put it simply, the more personal and important students perceive the material, the more positive their affective response.

Second, the teacher must be scientifically competent in the area being taught. The necessity of this component is obvious. Third, the teacher must also be educationally competent. While most science educators would include the former component as a "must," I contend that this component is also critical. I am, for example, a meteorology teacher. That task involves two disciplines: meteorology **and** education. Effective, quality teaching requires that I be competent in both, not just my science area.

Finally, a good teacher must have an appropriate "teaching personality." A somewhat nebulous component, admittedly, but mandatory nonetheless. Helpful ingredients would include enthusiasm (which is a highly contagious virus!), sense of humor, maintenance of a pleasant disposition, allowing the students to see you as a person (i.e, down and out of the ivory tower), and a genuine concern for students and their welfare--even on days when Attila the Hun would seem like a choirboy compared to the way you really feel!

Instruction in Music Must Follow Institutional Mission
By Sterling P. Cossaboom, Department of Music

The attempt of most music faculty to adhere to the traditional "conservatory" model abrogates the function of music in education in the university where the student population is significantly different. Consequently, it becomes the task and responsibility of the university music program to establish instructional objectives that provide students, irrespective of their musical backgrounds, a variety of musical experiences that will enable them to become conversant with the wide variety of musical languages and the origins of those languages as they are manifested in American music. As the music program develops in students an understanding of the "pluralistic" nature of musical traditions, the program can guide students on how the "aesthetic, social, political, religious, and philosophical" values of a culture are reflected in their music. Similarly, the program can help students create music, compose, improve or recreate, in a variety of traditions, including the contemporary use of electronic music technology.

These objectives may be attained through a variety of experiential formats applicable to traditional lecture, laboratory and activity courses, performing ensembles, studio instruction, and independent studies. Students should become involved in the creation of musics at a level concomitant with their musical development. For faculty to assist students to become creative they, themselves, must be immersed in the creative process.

If these are, indeed, the instructional objectives of the music program, then curriculum, faculty, and students can be measured as to the extent to which they meet these objectives. Since faculty are the role models and because it is the involvement of faculty in performance, composition and other creative scholarly activities that drives the music program, it is important to assess how effectively faculty meet the music program's instructional objectives. If, for example, an objective of the music program is "to develop a working knowledge of American Music," then the performance faculty should "perform" American Music, and composers should "compose" American Music, and all coursework should contain a component that addresses this objective. Faculty members should be reviewed in terms of these objectives.

Obviously, one needs to define the characteristics of "American Music," but it should be clear that if the performance faculty regularly and routinely perform works of nineteenth century European masters then their commitment to the instructional objective is questionable. Similarly, if the "research" of the musicology faculty involves the music of historical, non-American composers, then it is likely that the courses these faculty develop will reflect their research interests rather than the instructional objective.

It seems reasonable, then, that agreed-upon instructional objectives that reflect the role and mission of the university music program should form the basis of faculty creative and scholarly activity. Further, the results of faculty creative and scholarly activity should be manifested in the courses the faculty teach. Thus, the standard model is the teacher/performer. Such a person is both a strong producer of music and is accomplished as a classroom teacher. The benefits of the situation are substantial in that the teacher/performer has a life structured to provide time for performance uncompromised by commercial necessities and professional contact with bright and interested students.

"Faculty Practice:" Common to Various Forms in Nursing
by Janet Weber, Department of Nursing

The profession of nursing is both an art and an applied science. It differs from the pure sciences in that it is a practice discipline, in which patient care is a priority. Although nursing theory can be learned from a textbook, nursing practice cannot be learned in the same manner. Expert nursing role models are needed for students to learn the complex art of nursing. Therefore, nurse educators are encouraged to participate in some type of "faculty practice" to maintain professional competence which is necessary to provide effective nursing education.

"Faculty practice" can be broadly described as an interaction with patient situations in clinical settings. Nursing faculty cannot be expected to keep current in all areas of high-technical skills, but must be in frequent contact with practicing professionals to know what is credible and current in the real world. Faculty practice is an activity that enables faculty to practice what they teach students to do. Nursing educators may choose to engage in faculty practice in a variety of ways, which include clinical research, clinical nursing practice, and clinical consultation.

Clinical research is used to expand the scientific basis for nursing practice. Clinical nursing practice must be supported by theory and research. In turn, nursing theory and research must develop from nursing practice. Therefore, clinical nursing practice and nursing theory are interdependent. A faculty choosing to engage in clinical research may collaborate with practicing nurses to identify nursing practice problems in order to design and implement clinical research projects. The results of this research may be utilized to propose or support change in clinical practice areas. Collaboration with a nurse educator can enable these practicing nurses to engage in research studies that will answer questions related to patient care.

Another way to participate in faculty practice is by clinical nursing practice. Practicing as a nurse clinician can enable faculty to maintain excellence in their clinical skills through direct or indirect patient care. Patient care may be provided by teaching students in clinical areas, practicing in joint appointments with health care agencies, practicing through part-time employment, or by providing patient care in university based health clinics or day-care centers. Faculty may also elect to participate in private practice or pursue a nursing fellowship to update clinical skills and knowledge in a specialty area of their choice. Some schools of nursing have also developed nurse-practice centers where faculty and students provide patient care together. An example, might be a wellness-promotion health center where student and faculty participate in performing patient assessments and patient teaching.

Finally, clinical consultation by faculty can be used to assist nurses in professional practice. Nursing faculty may demonstrate their professional competency by serving as a nursing consultant for various types of health care agencies. Often, nursing faculty are called upon by practicing nurses and nursing administrators to share their expertise in different situations. For example, perhaps a clinical agency is admitting more elderly patients than it had in the past. That agency may need a nursing educator with a gerontology specialty to assess the current situation, make recommendations, and assist with the education of staff nurses in this area. Consulting and providing information to nursing staff results in a reciprocal flow of information which enhances the professional development of the faculty. Whatever form of "faculty practice" the nurse educator chooses, it must be utilized to enhance one's own professional development and classroom teaching.

LESSONS TO BE LEARNED

- A faculty member's effectiveness should be measured within the context of the mission of the institution.

- The application of a faculty member's philosophy of teaching should be used to guide the assessment process.

- Department and course objectives can be used to form the basis of a faculty assessment plan.

- Wide variations may occur in the assessment process between disciplines and within certain disciplines.

Maintaining Professional Competence

As already suggested, the examples provided in the preceding section illustrate the wide variance possible in assessing faculty performance. The objectives to be achieved, the strategies to be employed, and the measures to be evaluated all impact on the resulting teacher scholar model. In a similar vein, how a faculty member goes about maintaining his/her currency can also influence the resulting structures.

So often the assessment of a faculty member tends to focus primarily on "what is produced." What are the scholarly accomplishments? What gains have been demonstrated by the students? What evidence can be provided that changes have occurred? Clearly, the assessment movement has propelled this perspective to new heights of importance. Historically, and even more so now, the so-called "input measures" have received limited attention. While the Ph.D. has been the standard bearer of the input measures perspective, the review of course planning efforts, organization of content, development of instructional materials, and the study of instructional strategies have not been foremost in either assessment or evaluation models.

Likewise, little consideration has been given to what professors actually do to maintain professional competence as a means to demonstrate their effectiveness. The approaches used by faculty to maintain competence provide some insights into the type of evidence that may be collected in the evaluative process. On occasion, one might be asked to provide a self-assessment, but typically these efforts focus on the traditional measures of effectiveness. If developmental activities are to be valued and these behaviors provide an indication of what faculty members do, it only makes sense that evidence related to staying current be considered in the evaluation process. How else would one suggest that these behaviors be encouraged?

The approaches used by faculty to maintain competence should provide some insights into the type of evidence that may be collected in the evaluative process.

Again, to generate new ways of thinking about this question, faculty colleagues in the sample were given some leading questions:

- How do you stay up-to-date and current in your discipline?
- What do you do to stay professionally active?
- How do you improve your teaching ability?
- What kinds of activities stimulate your professional development?

The responses to these questions suggest specific ways in which faculty perform-ance may be judged within this new context.

Staying Competent in Political Science
by Peter J. Bergerson, Department of Political Science

There are three ways a faculty member can stay current. First, he/she must be current and up-to-date on discipline innovations which can be integrated into the content and teaching of a course. Within political science, there are a number of ways this can be accomplished. Professional publications, such as **The Political Science Teacher**, offer a faculty member the opportunity for a wealth of new ideas to keep current and up-to-date.

An additional source for ideas to be "current and up-to-date" are confer-ence workshops, seminars which are devoted exclusively to teaching new ideas. For example, the National Conference on Teaching Public Policy and Adminis-tration is an invaluable source of inspiration, ideas, and energy for integrating scholarship and teaching. I have used a number of the papers from this conference in my classes such as simulations, structured trips, and the use of community resource people.

Second, faculty members must act; they must take the ideas and new approaches learned from above and incorporate them into their classes. One approach is to integrate reading (textbook) and lecture with active student learning. For example, the introductory political science class has a section on "public opinion, the media, and polling." The students could develop a poll and as a team project survey political opinion of individuals in the community. This would make for a stimulating and challenging section of the course. Additional active learning exercises could include attending a trial. I have found that attending the opening or closing arguments of a trial are excellent learning opportunities for the students when discussing the judicial system. I have also conducted a mock trial with the students as a learning device. In my class on government budgeting, I have found simulation of a budget hearing as a way to generate student learning. Each student selects a government agency and prepares a budget for the next fiscal year. The class serves as the appropriations committee of the legislature. Each student must present and defend his/her budget to the class.

Third, participation in the political and the governmental process can be a measure of professional competence. I have been very active in both the politics of the Southeast Missouri area as well as the administration of local governments. On the political scene, I have conducted polls, written speeches, and provided campaign and election advice. I am frequently called on for advice on the probability of a particular candidate winning an election, or what are the prospects of a particular issue (i.e., a tax issue) being successful in the polls.

Furthermore, I have been active in the administration and management of municipal government over the past ten years. I serve as a resource person and consultant to the City Managers Association of Southeast Missouri. In addition, I have been regularly called on for professional advice by area municipalities. I have provided research and advice on such issues as personnel problems and at-large versus ward elections.

Currency of the Teacher-Philosopher
by Dennis Holt, Department of Philosophy and Religion

Professional competence in philosophy is not exactly equivalent to staying up-to-date with the latest research. Philosophy is not a field in which widely accepted advances accumulate and become a common foundation for new investigations. Yet active philosophers have philosophical interests which they pursue through reading and writing. They acquaint themselves with the latest literature relevant to their interests and they seek out colleagues, students, and others with whom to share and test their ideas.

I take teaching seriously; and this, rather than the production of original work in philosophy, is my primary professional intent. To remain vital as a teacher I make it a rule never to be satisfied. Teaching is something that takes place between me and my students. Faced with glassy-eyed students, I can choose to ignore their disengagement or to see it as their fault. On the other hand, I can choose to look at factors that are within my control: I can alter my teaching style; I can restructure my assignments; I can examine my expectations. For help there are numerous resources available. There is a rapidly expanding literature on teaching in higher education. I read **College Teaching** and **Teaching Philosophy**, and have also found specialty journals in other disciplines to be helpful. When I try new ideas, I share them with my colleagues. And my colleagues share their ideas with me. There is no better antidote to complacency and mediocrity than informal discussion among departmental colleagues who care about philosophy and teaching. I have also benefitted from discussions with colleagues outside of philosophy, especially from the insights of our faculty development expert, the Director of the Center for Teaching and Learning. Student evaluations seldom give me specific information in terms of which I can improve my teaching, but they affirm my own perceptions and in that sense provide a basis for cultivating my teaching skills.

If my profession is teaching philosophy, it is as a philosopher that I teach. Professors of history had better speak to their student as historians--even if it is not their lot to produce original work in the field. This kind of professional activity cannot be conducted in isolation; hence, it is necessary not only to read but also to write, talk, and listen to philosophy. I make it a practice to read much more deeply and broadly in a subject matter than my students could ever be expected to do in a single semester. For example, in a new course on self and authenticity, I will need to say something about Hegel. Though I could pass on relevant insights to my students from a readily available secondary source, it would be unprofessional to do so without having surveyed both primary and secondary sources generally. This kind of research is then integrated into a view of the subject matter, recorded in notes and class handouts, that reflect my own professional judgment. In fashioning this view, I don't rise to the level of making original contributions to Hegel scholarship or the philosophy of human nature, but I do develop myself professionally as a philosopher.

At some point one must submit one's ideas to the critique of other philosophers. There are several ways of doing this. The approach taken by Socrates was to get together with other sharp minds and argue. (Socrates challenged ideas in the agora; academic philosophers often meet in the hallway outside the open door of a colleague's office, in the coffee room, or, more formally, in a seminar room.) Another approach is to share short papers, class handouts, and notes with colleagues for criticism and response. And, of course, one can learn a lot from attending professional conferences, participating in special interest sessions, reading papers, writing book reviews, and submitting papers for publication.

Staying Current and Up-to-Date in Speech
by Thomas Harte, Department of Speech Communication and Theatre

Maintaining professional competence has two dimensions: (1) staying up-to-date in your subject matter field, and (2) improving teaching skills and methodologies. There are three activities that are indispensable to maintaining my currency in the field. Though hardly novel, the frequent reading of professional journals and attendance at professional meetings are two fundamental prerequisites. The third is a little more distinctive. Every professor needs to be involved in an ongoing "project." It need not be something destined for publication. (In fact, there is a danger, I think, in placing too much emphasis on a project's potential for publication rather than on its usefulness to the teacher.) It might be something aimed solely at the classroom, such as developing a new unit, collecting new resource materials, or experimenting with different teaching methods.

Most of what I know about teaching has come from formal and informal interactions with other teachers. Thus, I believe a university should do everything it can to encourage such exchanges. The following four illustrations provide a starting point for such activity.

Mentoring programs. My first college-level teaching job found me back on the campus where I had been an undergraduate. Thus, it was perfectly natural for me to ask my colleagues (most of them former teachers) for help. Moreover, as an assistant debate coach I served what amounted to an apprenticeship. But I suspect that today many novice teachers would think twice about seeking such assistance for fear that they will somehow reveal weakness or lack of preparation. Mentoring programs benefit both parties in the relationship and ought to be encouraged and rewarded.

Team teaching. I have found few things more valuable than collaborating with a colleague, whether less experienced or more experienced than I. Though we generally tend to think of team teaching arrangements in terms of an entire class for a full semester, there are many ways to implement collaboration short of that. For example, a single unit might be shared. Two colleagues might get together to construct a mutual examination, lead a discussion, or give a lecture. Or they might read papers or listen to speeches submitted by the other's students.

Auditing colleagues. Taking someone else's course is a valuable way to get back in touch with the perspective of the student and to generate insights into effective teaching strategies. The person being audited benefits too, both from the discussions that inevitably take place after each class session as well as from the incentive to do the very best job in front of a colleague.

Regular and systematic review. Every hospital has a review board which meets regularly to discuss important or difficult cases. If what I see each week on "L.A. Law" is any indication, it is likewise typical for partners in a law firm to meet regularly to confer over cases. But nothing quite like this exists at the university. Indeed, there are few if any systematic opportunities for faculty members to sit around a table to report what progress they are making in the classroom or to seek advice and counsel. Everyone would probably benefit if we in academia adopted the approach of most businesses and organizations and set aside regular time periods to collectively take stock of what we are doing on the job, i.e., in the classroom.

LESSONS TO BE LEARNED

- Staying up-to-date with the literature and current practices in the field are critical factors to be measured in the evaluative process.

- Alternative measures of professional competence are needed to effectively evaluate the extent to which faculty members are "practicing their art."

- Professional organizations provide a broad array of experiences that may be used to assess professional currency.

- Professional engagement with colleagues affords numerous opportunities for assessment and enhancement of professional competencies.

- Systematic assessment and review procedures are fundamental to the development of ongoing evaluation processes.

Demonstrating Professional Competence

In each of the preceding sections, implications have been made and insights suggested that have significant potential for altering the ways in which faculty members consider the importance of what they actually do as teacher scholars. The task is to translate these activities into tangible alternatives that can be used to form an expanded evaluative base for measuring faculty performance. Once accomplished, individual campuses need only determine the appropriate level of attention (value) that should be given to these alternatives and the traditionally defined measures. What is the appropriate balance?

In concluding their assignment, the faculty members focused specifically on alternatives that might be used to construct such a framework. The guiding questions were similar to these issues already raised:

- What are the other ways in which your technical/content expertise can be demonstrated?
- How many different ways can you identify? Describe.
- Are there any approaches unique to your discipline? If so, what?
- How can research on teaching be used to enhance your professional competence?

The task is to translate these activities into tangible alternatives that can be used to form an expanded evaluative base for measuring faculty performance.

Literature Professor Reflects on Teaching and Scholarship
by Robert W. Hamblin, Department of English

As one who spends a good part of his professional life researching/ reflecting, writing, and publishing, I am not inclined to discount such activities as a legitimate means of demonstrating professional competence. In fact, though I eschew the "publish or perish" syndrome, I believe that the traditional expectation that teachers/scholars should do a basic amount of publishing is altogether fair and appropriate. The problem should not be viewed as "either-or" but rather "both-and": that is, how to create and maintain a healthy balance between the two separate but related activities so that each can feed into and enhance the other.

Having made this claim, however, I will gladly go on to concede that the traditional emphasis upon publication is not the **only** means of gauging a faculty member's worth as a scholar/researcher. Surprisingly, though, for a profession that prides itself upon originality, innovation, and adaptability, higher education has not been very imaginative or creative in identifying other criteria by which to judge professional competence. While I would not claim to have all, or even the best, solutions to the problem, I do have a few convictions about the direction we should go.

First of all, we must develop means of encouraging and supporting post-graduate (including post-doctoral) study. If we truly believe that learning is an ongoing process, even lifelong, then we should quit talking so much about "terminal" degrees. Even Ph.D.'s can reasonably be expected to upgrade their knowledge and skills, perhaps even resume formal study, from time to time.

I do not mean to imply that what is needed is merely stacking up additional levels of formal education beyond the Ph.D.--the Ph.D. plus 15 hours, say, or the Ph.D. plus 30. I am not opposed to such an approach in those cases in which an institution and an individual faculty member agree that additional hours would be mutually beneficial, but I would prefer a much more flexible system. One practical possibility is for each faculty member (tenured as well as non-tenured) to develop, in consultation with his or her department chairperson and dean, to develop an individual portfolio of projected activities that would both demonstrate and enhance professional competence. This portfolio, which should be revised every three-to-five years, might include seminars, institutes, faculty exchanges, independent studies, consultations, and travel, as well as formal course credit and/or research/writing projects. In every case the portfolios should be developed around both institutional and individual needs and interests.

Another possibility is to develop and perfect tools to assess classroom performance and learning outcomes. I am not as enamored as some of exit testing, since, like most educators, I tend to believe (at least hope) that the impact upon students' lives of what I teach does not conclude on the day of the final examination. The ultimate test of any teacher is how well or how poorly his/her students turn out in later years. Still, if combined with other means of evaluation, exit tests and other outcome assessment measures can be very useful. I support student evaluations of professors and classes, peer reviews by colleagues and administrators, and course and program assessments and believe that information gathered from these sources should weigh heavily in decisions regarding promotion and retention of faculty.

Finally, I also believe that a professor's scholarly abilities can be judged in large part on the kinds of activities incorporated into the course content. Recognizing the crucial function as role model for students, the genuine scholar will seek to ground his/her courses in the research methods of inquiry, search, assimilation, and critical response. Such a professor will view the library as an adjunct classroom; he/she will utilize the library holdings as an expanded textbook.

I seek to teach my students that education, rightly understood, is not a body of knowledge (cannot be, since that body of knowledge is ever changing) but rather a **process** of exploration and discovery: always exciting, unpredictable, challenging (especially to old ideas), and never ending. Research, therefore, is not tangential to learning and education--something that professors do in their spare time instead of playing golf; on the contrary, it is one of the essential skills that students need to master in order to become successful and productive individuals, workers, and citizens.

The Field-Based Elementary Education Teacher Scholar
by Sandra L. Renegar, Department of Elementary and Special Education

My objective as a teacher educator is to effect a change in behavior through enhanced knowledge. Obviously, measuring this objective is more difficult than counting publications and/or presentations or totaling grant dollars. Certainly, publications and presentations are avenues for sharing information about changes in teaching behaviors I have helped initiate. The volume of articles published annually in education is enormous; many of these contribute nothing to the knowledge base and often represent shoddy efforts at research. Thus, merely adding to this body of publications may provide no indications of a faculty member's professional competence. Since the population most impacted by my competence consists primarily of elementary educators, those are the professionals who serve as important judges in measuring my effectiveness.

As my undergraduates engage in their initial teaching experiences in public school classrooms, I work closely with the cooperating teachers in the field. These people see my students in the "real world" setting more than I do. I meet with them regularly to ascertain the strengths and weaknesses demonstrated by the university students. If many of these teachers voiced concerns frequently, I would know I have not adequately prepared my students for their responsibilities in the field. If problems occurred with an isolated student, my effectiveness as a field supervisor could be determined by the success of my intervention with the student. A subjective measure of my professional competence in this role could be obtained through the administration of an evaluation instrument to be completed by teachers and administrators in the schools where my students were placed. Data gathered from the students' completion of the instrument also yields some insight about the effectiveness of my performance.

At the graduate level, most of my students are public school teachers with varying amounts of professional experience. I have used several strategies to attempt to help these students enhance their teaching skills. One strategy places me in the role of information dispenser; in others, I serve more as a facilitator. When I lecture, I share information based on research wherever possible. One example of this information causing change to occur involves research on spelling instruction. After describing and demonstrating the self-corrected test and test-study-test methods, many of my students change their spelling instruction to try these methods. One teacher said she had changed her spelling instruction to include the self-corrected test and test-study-test methods and her students also improved their spelling scores. Several others chimed in that they, too, had experienced similar success. Information I dispensed had enabled these teachers to enhance their teaching effectiveness. These teachers could provide evidence that my professional competence had enabled them to improve their own classroom teaching.

When I serve as a facilitator of change, I provide a general framework for students to design their own project. In my classes dealing with a specific content area, students implement action research in their own classrooms. Students base their action research on experimental research cited in educational literature. This hard data provides the rationale for their projects. Students conduct their action research for the period of time most appropriate to their classroom situation and document its effect on student performance in the specified content/skill area. Again, assessment of their projects might suggest further change in their teaching behaviors.

Another example of validation of my professional competence comes from the requests I receive for informal consultation. The Missouri Department of Elementary and Secondary Education awards grant money to public school teachers submitting meritorious grant proposals. Teachers who are my former students call me for information as they prepare these proposals. All of these inquiries give evidence that my public school colleagues respect my knowledge and abilities. Again, quantification is difficult but public school educators could assist in validation of my professional competence.

Home Economics Professor Steps Outside the Classroom

By Shelba Branscum, Department of Human Environmental Studies

As a professor of home economics, I teach courses in the areas of family, marriage, human sexuality, and parent education. These subject matter areas require an educational philosophy which contends that learning is a dynamic human process which necessitates the active involvement of the professor, as well as the student, and the learning environment. I am a learning facilitator first and foremost. The teaching environment is as important as the concepts and factual entities of the discipline.

Staying current in any field of study is a difficult task. For me it is particularly important that I work closely with professionals in agencies, organizations, and programs that target human services. In addition to some of the traditional measures of excellence, the following activities illustrate alternative indicators that can be used to demonstrate my professional competence: 1) Testify in a court of law involving expert testimony regarding the care and disposition of children who are involved in child abuse or custody hearings; 2) Provide testimony at hearings conducted by the state legislature regarding the development of new state laws in child care licensure, family rights, and nursing home residence rights as expert contribution; 3) Participate in community and state task force committees, i.e., Governor's Task Force, County Senior Service Fund Board of Directors; 4) Provide technical assistance in setting up academic programs at other institutions; 5) Serve on accreditation teams for Head Start Regional Programs as monitored by the Department of Health, Education, and Welfare; 6) Develop curriculum guides, workbooks for university classes, resource manuals and networking guides for community and classroom use; 7) Recognition by professional organizations for service and contribution to the field of study; 8) Consultant for community service organizations, i.e., nursing homes, day care centers, board of directors for mental health organizations; and 9) Lead and conduct workshops and seminars for professionals in the field as inservice training, i.e., geriatric social workers, nurses, and psychologists at Farmington Mental Hospital, or regional family service administrators and supervisors in the state.

Remaining active in the field and community, coupled with current academic preparation are the two most important activities I am involved in professionally. Research is an important activity which must be conducted from time to time in order to contribute to the body of knowledge. My efforts in professional development have consistently reflected the strength in my style of teaching as well as the demands in the professional discipline.

Measures of Competence in Chemistry Come From Many Sources

by Mike Readnour, Department of Chemistry

There are many ways, in addition to publishing, that chemistry faculty members can demonstrate their professional competence. One way is to serve as a consultant to an organization that needs chemical expertise. For example, I have served for several years as an item writer for the Medical College Admission test (MCAT). This exam is taken by each student seeking admission to a medical school in the United States. Being an item writer for the MCAT requires that I keep my knowledge of chemistry current.

The American Chemical Society (ACS) is the national professional organization for chemists. In 1983, I organized the Southeast Missouri Chemistry Bowl, which is a joint venture of the chemistry department at Southeast Missouri State and the local section of ACS. The high school competition consists of a 35-question, multiple choice exam and two laboratory experiments. Also, ACS has several national committees working on curricular matters and ways of improving the teaching of chemistry. I served for ten years on the General Chemistry Test Committee of the Division of Chemical Education of the American Chemical Society. This committee is responsible for developing a standardized examination covering one year of college general chemistry. Being a part of these activities helps keep me abreast of recent developments in the field of chemistry.

Since chemistry is a laboratory science, chemistry faculty are continuously involved in laboratory activities. The chemistry faculty in our department have developed many laboratory innovations. These include video taping laboratory techniques and instructions for particular laboratory experiments and creating new laboratory experiments. One of my colleagues recently developed a thin layer chromatography experiment to separate and identify the dyes that are contained within various types of ink. The experiment has gained national recognition and was published in the **Journal of Chemical Education**.

The computer skills that several of our faculty have are a tremendous asset to our program. Computer programs have been written to analyze data and make calculations. Another colleague has developed three microcomputer based laboratory experiments using the Apple IIe computer for one of our introductory chemistry courses. He has also interfaced an Apple II+ computer with an activity chamber to monitor activity levels in mice who have been administered a drug.

Another way of demonstrating professional competence is to become involved in the development of curricular materials for high school and elementary school science courses. Several members of the university science faculty participated in the Kindergarten through Sixth Science and Math (KSAM) project. The KSAM project is a science curriculum for elementary students. Members of the KSAM project met in small groups and wrote science lessons to address "key skills" that had been identified statewide as science skills that elementary students need to attain.

Chemistry classes can serve as "laboratories" for conducting studies that will help teachers increase the student learning that takes place in their courses. I recently carried out an investigation in my General Chemistry course to determine whether certain concepts of chemistry must be learned before other concepts or principles can be learned. Students were tested on the designated concepts and principles as part of the regular exams in the course. Analysis of the data taken in this investigation suggests that there are indeed certain fundamental concepts (e.g., the mole concept) which must be learned before other concepts and principles can be learned. I've tried to find ways to more effectively teach these fundamental concepts because they are so critical to other learning.

Broadly Defined Scholarship in Psychology
by Phillip Finney, Department of Psychology

Five dimensions of academic scholarship can be exhibited by psychologists. One of these dimensions, the standard demonstration of scholarship through research and publication, will not be detailed here. Instead, my focus will be on the remaining four dimensions. These are scholarship as a professional activity, engagement with the novel, community service, and pedagogy.

Professional activity. Scholarship as a professional activity refers to professional service to one's discipline. This service is shown through membership in professional associations, review of scholarly submissions, and presentation of colloquia.

Membership in professional associations is basic evidence of peer acceptance of a psychologist's professional ability and activity. Even more demonstrative of professional acceptance is leadership within organizations. The review of scholarly submissions of other psychologists includes the review of submissions to professional journals, grant agencies, and professional meetings. Prepublication review of textbooks or presubmission review of a colleague's research manuscript are other examples of creditable professional review. Invitation to make presentations of colloquia to faculty or students at the faculty member's own institution or at other academic institutions similarly provides another form of evidence of peer endorsement of one's competence.

Engagement of the novel. Engagement of the novel recognizes creativity as a demonstration of professional competence. Examples of professional creativity for a psychologist include: developing a new research methodology or technique; writing computer software that could be used in computerized research or in simulation studies; and developing a new approach to therapy or to consultation in a particular area. The distinguishing characteristic of engagement with the novel is that it extends other forms of scholarship beyond their current limits.

Community service. Community service that effectively uses one's professional skills reflects the significance and underlying competence of those skills. Community service also can cause a psychologist to explore new literature or methodologies to solve problems that had not been faced previously. Examples of such activity include: a clinical psychologist who engages in private practice that utilizes and sharpens professional skills; a developmental or clinical psychologist who participates in consultations in school systems or in other social agencies; a social psychologist who conducts marketing research for local businesses or who assists attorneys in jury selection and as an expert witness (e.g., on eyewitness accuracy); an environmental psychologist who assists in the planning of the design of buildings and offices or who assists in community planning.

Pedagogy. Most examples of scholarship through pedagogy can be seen as activities that a teacher might normally be expected to pursue. Still, these activities both reflect and extend the teacher's competence in the field. Exemplary activities include: major participation in curriculum revision; development of new or revised syllabi for new or old courses; development of new lectures for new or existing courses; and textbook writing. These activities are particularly effective in maintaining a psychologist's competence when they involve extensive reading and library research. A representative list would include: guest lectures in another faculty member's course; presentation of a colloquium that informs colleagues of new developments in the presenter's field of specialization; invitation of colleagues to attend and react to class presentations; development of instructional materials and techniques (e.g., computer simulations or exercises for students); and serving as a mentor for student research.

The list of activities covered by these four dimensions of scholarship suggests that almost any professional work by a psychologist can contribute to professional competence and, ultimately, to teaching effectiveness. Still, the same work, although improving professional competence, may not be relevant to teaching effectiveness. The critical factor is whether or not the individual applies his/her professional activity to the classroom setting.

LESSONS TO BE LEARNED

- There is a long list of untapped alternatives that might be used to demonstrate a faculty member's professional competence.

- A broad array of evaluative evidence is needed to effectively judge the professional competence of a faculty member.

- Professional colleagues, outside the academy, serve as an important source of evidence to evaluate the effectiveness of faculty members.

- Student evaluations, insights, and learning outcome measures serve an integral role in the evaluation process.

- Explorations into innovative, novel, and non-traditional areas serve as visible sources of scholarly investigation.

- The classroom serves as a major reservoir of evidence to demonstrate professional competence.

- The scholarly pursuit of pedagogy can be measured in a variety of different ways.

The full range of faculty responsibility extends far beyond the limited scope of traditional evaluative measures.

From these essays, it is easy to see there are various ways in which faculty performance might be judged. The shared insights illustrate the extremely narrow perspective of measuring faculty performance solely on the bases of the number of presentations made, articles published, and grants received. The full range of faculty responsibility extends far beyond the limited scope of such traditional evaluative measures. Teaching objectives and strategies provide context for the assessment process. Clearly, there are alternatives that are discipline based. Even within disciplines, wide variations might occur. And finally, what faculty members actually do to maintain and demonstrate their professional competence suggests broad new insights into how the evaluation process might be tailored around what professors actually do. The task ahead is to translate these indicators into evaluation structures.

The opportunities for reform suggested by the rethinking of the basic assessment process require action on all levels. The answers to the questions raised are vested with the faculty. Institutional leaders need to capitalize on these insights to create a new future. These challenges must be addressed by all members of the academic community.

The answers to the questions raised are vested with the faculty. Institutional leaders need to capitalize on these insights to create a new future.

Actions

Premise

Change requires leadership that is action-oriented.

Challenge

To implement change, leaders must:
- Chart specific actions
- Guide reform processes
- Address leadership challenges

CHAPTER 7

CHARTING NEW DIRECTIONS

The task of elevating the status of teaching, implementing the teacher scholar concept, and developing an evaluation process that integrates the wholeness of the teaching/learning process is a challenge that impacts the entire academy. Obviously, this change initiative cannot be achieved without the direct intervention by administrators throughout the nation's higher education establishment. Administrators and faculty members alike must work together to achieve mutually acceptable goals. Individual biases will need to be set aside so efforts can be directed toward constructive solutions. The current "new born state of readiness" provides a positive context in which the reform can occur. Academic leaders must seize this opportunity. They must assume a leadership posture that forces individuals throughout the academy to rethink basic processes and to chart new directions. The time has come for leaders to demonstrate:

> *1) [A] firm expression of the importance of teaching; 2) a willingness to marshall resources to support excellence in the classroom; 3) an ability to lead a campus-wide initiative to change existing attitudes, perceptions, and, in some cases, procedures; 4) an ability to build bonds and linkages between administrative personnel and faculty colleagues; and 5) a willingness to develop a plan of action that provides the basis for a consistent and sustained campus-wide effort. The opportunity for substantive change is squarely before the academic community; the leadership challenge must be accepted by academic leaders across the nation! (5:43)*

In an earlier publication, entitled **Administrative Commitment to Teaching**, the author addressed the breadth of the challenge ahead by identifying five major areas in which planned action must occur:

- Campus Environment and Culture
- Employment Policies and Practices
- Strategic Administrative Actions
- Instructional Enhancement Efforts
- Instructional Development Activities

The current "new born state of readiness" provides a positive context in which the reform can occur. Academic leaders must seize the opportunity.

These areas serve as the five major headings of this chapter. In each section, practical examples are given on how the reform challenges can be met. More specific action-oriented illustrations for each area are identified in the Workshop Supplement, pages 149-165. The research base for these change initiatives was derived by the author from a 1987 national survey of chief academic officers in the nation's four-year degree granting institutions. The respondent group of 1328 chief academic officers represented 65.4 percent of the nation's academic leaders. The complete analysis of this research, including a breakdown by size of institutions is included in **Administrative Commitment to Teaching**.

This research also reaffirmed that the demands for reform are not limited to those outside of higher education or those in the faculty ranks. The data indicate that chief academic officers themselves are not satisfied with the levels of institutional commitment to instructional effectiveness. In fact, when respondents were asked to rate twenty-five items on a scale of 1 (low) to 10 (high) only six items received a rating of 8.0 or above. A general analysis of the perceptions of these chief academic officers reveals that there are significant differences in the levels of institutional commitment within the various areas. These distinctions are particularly noteworthy and vividly illustrate that efforts made to elevate teaching must be appropriately tailored action by action and campus to campus. Different levels of activity will be needed if a campus is to effectively implement the desired reforms. Furthermore, the overall data from the study indicate that broad generalizations to re-emphasize teaching or singular efforts to "change the system" will not likely create the type of reform that will be needed. Changing the level of commitment to teaching is a more complex task than it may appear on the surface.

Broad generalizations to re-emphasize teaching or singular efforts to "change the system" will not likely create the type of reform that will be needed. Changing the level of commitment to teaching is a more complex task than it may appear on the surface.

One of the most important factors in any change initiative is to determine the level of satisfaction or uneasiness experienced by those who must assume a major leadership role in the change process. If leaders are, in fact, happy or pleased with the current situation, the likelihood of their advocating change is greatly diminished. Conversely, a relatively high level of administrative discontentment may suggest a high level of readiness to press forward with substantial modification of existing patterns.

The data from the chief academic officers suggest that several areas exist where their level of satisfaction is quite low. In fact, even in the highest rated area, employment policies and practices, the 7.7 mean score on a ten-point scale is not

Table 1
Ratings of Chief Academic Officers' Satisfaction Levels with Institutional Performance by Instructional Improvement Category (5:40)

Category	Percentage by Level of Rating										Mean
	1	2	3	4	5	6	7	8	9	10	
Employment Policies and Practices	1	1	2	4	6	8	13	27	25	14	**7.7**
Campus Environment and Culture	1	1	3	4	9	13	20	25	16	8	**7.1**
Strategic Administrative Action	0	3	5	7	11	14	19	22	14	5	**6.7**
Instructional Enhancement Efforts	3	5	7	11	14	13	17	18	7	3	**5.8**
Instructional Development Activities	6	9	14	12	11	11	17	13	5	2	**5.2**

overpowering. Table 1 presents the percentage of chief academic officers' ratings of the five categories according to their grouping on the ten-point rating scale. It indicates, for example, that 14 percent of the academic leaders give the employment policies and practices category a rating of 10, whereas only 2 percent gave instructional development activities a 10 rating. The clustering of double digit percentage responses further illustrates the descending level of satisfaction within the five areas.

These generic areas suggest the broad latitude for actions that might occur to reinforce the importance of teaching. The implementation of the teacher scholar concept must be a focal point of discussions and activities centered under the area of employment policies and practices. The total campus-wide perspective, however, cannot be ignored. Only through the development of a broad-based set of institutional initiatives can the full impact of the reform be achieved. Change must be forthcoming from all segments of the academy.

Only through the development of a broad-based set of institutional initiatives can the full impact of the reform be achieved. Change must be forthcoming from all segments of the academy.

Campus Environment and Culture

The last two decades have witnessed a substantial growth in the volume of literature dedicated to the field of organizational behavior. In higher education, the area has had an even more recent surge of interest. Clearly, the "institutional quality of life" has an impact on the overall learning atmosphere on campus. This environment may be shaped by longstanding traditions, administrative actions, leadership styles, printed materials, and various forms of communication.

On a daily basis, numerous factors impinge upon the development of a positive campus environment. All too often, however, what typically gets attention on most campuses are negative events, actions, or rumors. Concerns over enrollment, resource allocations, promotion decisions, and a multitude of distracting elements often force teaching excellence to go unnoticed. These issues are compounded, too, by the very nature of some faculty members, whose background and preparation to analyze, probe, and question often seem to convey a negative perspective. The creation of a positive teaching/learning environment thus requires constant attention.

Beyond the classroom and the competency of the individual faculty member, there are several indicators that may be used to assess the general supportive nature of the campus teaching environment. One's level of security, sense of institutional pride, personal ownership in campus activities, perceptions about administrative leadership, and intellectual vitality all contribute to this sense of community. Faculty responses to a few basic questions can suggest an overall feeling of this campus tone. Do the campus structures provide for open debate and dialogue? Is there a high level of pride in the institution's academic standards and a strong commitment to students, quality of teaching and scholarship, and its programs? Are there research, scholarly, and creative activities under way that stimulate classroom instruction?

To provide more specific indicators of the impact of selected campus perspectives, the chief academic officers that responded in the above study were asked to respond on the ten-point scale to five statements. Table 2 indicates that they see current efforts as only moderately successful in sustaining a positive environment that is supportive of teaching.

Table 2
Perceived Commitment of the Campus Environment and Culture in Support of Instructional Effectiveness (5:49)

Items	% Rating 1, 2 or 3	Mean	% Rating 8, 9 or 10
Faculty have a clear sense of ownership of the curriculum and other instructional concerns	2	**8.3**	74
There is a shared feeling of institutional pride that stimulates effective classroom performance	5	**7.4**	56
The level of intellectual vitality and morale on campus is conducive to effective instruction	3	**7.3**	53
There is a clear sense of administrative stability that allows faculty to focus on the instructional process	8	**7.1**	53
The faculty have a clear sense of confidence in the upper administrative leadership that fosters effective instruction	7	**6.9**	43

The item regarding faculty ownership of the curriculum (mean = 8.3) ranked as the fourth highest item out of the twenty-five statements in the survey. Seventy-four percent of the chief academic officers placed this item in the good/excellent category rating of 8, 9 or 10. This is the only item in this category that was within the good/excellent range (8 or above).

A review of each of these five areas suggests numerous ways in which the professoriate can respond in a constructive manner. Action-oriented illustrations in these areas are identified on pages 149-152. They emphasize that there are numerous low cost initiatives that might be pursued to improve the campus level of support for teaching excellence. The required level of commitment and energy greatly outweighs the amount of dollars that must be spent.

The required level of commitment and energy greatly outweighs the amount of dollars that must be spent.

Faculty Ownership. Like most professionals, faculty members exhibit strong tendencies to be an integral part of their institution. The structure of the academy, however, produces numerous forces that naturally work against these normal instincts. Disciplinary and departmental pressures push faculty members to pursue narrow areas of specialization. The competitive nature of grants and research often motivate faculty members to pursue personal rather than collaborative goals. And, often, the sheer size of some universities promotes the development of subcultures. Yet, most faculty members have a strong overriding sense of identity with their campus. There is a striving for a sense of community and a desire to be a part of the whole.

While the faculty generally have a strong sense of curricular ownership, it deserves an even higher level of support. The placement of increased attention here can be used as an effective illustration of a strong commitment to the implementation of a teacher scholar model. Actions are needed that facilitate dialogue, promote the application of high standards, and stimulate faculty-based program initiatives.

Institutional Pride. There are numerous sources that may be used to create a sense of institutional pride. Typically, academic quality and successes are primary forces that support a strong feeling of pride among the various campus constituencies. There are also close connections that exist between teaching and institutional pride. If, for example, there is a strong sense of pride, faculty members will likely expect more from students and give more in the classroom setting. They will regularly communicate positive images to others who in turn will feel better about the institution and promote its successes. The data collected from the chief academic officers suggest that the difficulty in achieving these goals increases with the size of the campus.

Regardless of institutional size, executive and academic leaders can have a significant impact on the sense of campus pride. Their personal examples and commitment to excellence can greatly foster such feelings. A positive teaching/ learning atmosphere can be enhanced by actions that develop a sense of ownership, convey a customer service orientation, and positively promote the quality of the institution.

Intellectual Vitality. Intellectual vitality is one of the most important characteristics of an outstanding faculty member. Stressing the importance of teaching does not lessen the need for faculty members to be active, practicing scholars. Nor does it suggest that research and creative endeavors are unimportant. To the contrary, teaching excellence demands disciplinary competence. If anything, the elevated status of teaching only suggests the need to broaden the means of evaluating teaching and measuring one's intellectual vitality.

Faculty morale can significantly influence the overall instructional environment of a campus. It can be a deterrent to productive scholarship and can contribute negatively to changes that might otherwise be perceived as positive accomplishment. As an example, placing more emphasis on teaching may be perceived by some as changing the rules, thereby having a negative effect on their morale. Institutional leaders need to deal effectively with campus-wide concerns, maintain open communication channels, and stimulate the pursuit of outstanding classroom excellence.

Administrative Stability. Providing a consistent message, maintaining an ongoing level of commitment, and providing a sense of common direction are obvious requirements to sustain any initiative. This clarity of purpose may be of even greater importance to changing the status of teaching since it is often placed in the "assumed category." New campus projects and priorities can send mixed signals, particularly if they are not connected with planned objectives. Similarly, high turnover rates among chief academic officers (now less than a four-year average) make it almost impossible to provide the sustained type of leadership needed to implement substantive reform. The moderately positive assessments in this area as suggested in Table 2 illustrate the need for strong leadership in this area. Steps need to be taken to ensure institutional continuity. Actions that reinforce the evolutionary nature of change, maintain a sense of planned change, and integrate the role of teaching into formal policy statements can be used to give greater stability to the campus.

Administrative Leadership. Administrative leadership is the easiest, most identifiable element that can be singled out in assessing the campus environment. The type of initiatives proposed, the manner in which decisions are made, the degree to which collegial actions are taken, and the overall approach to decision making, all contribute to the sense of community. Taking strong positions on the importance of teaching is essential to the emergence of an operational definition of a teacher scholar model. Academic and executive leaders need to take actions that stimulate effective instruction and promote a more receptive learning atmosphere.

Strong leadership initiatives can create a more positive teaching/learning environment. Initiatives and plans for action need not be elaborate or detailed. They do, however, need to be focused on teaching and sustained over a long period of time. The examples and illustrations provided in the Workshop Supplement section suggest a framework that can sustain leadership in the areas of faculty ownership, institutional pride, intellectual vitality, administrative stability, and leadership. Administrative actions can promote a strong teaching culture. Little can be achieved, however, in isolation; teaching must be made a campus-wide priority.

Administrative actions can promote a strong teaching culture. Little can be achieved, however, in isolation; teaching must be made a campus-wide priority.

Employment Policies and Practices

Each of the preceding chapters has directly emphasized and indirectly referenced areas that have specific implications for changes that must be forthcoming in the full range of employment-related functions. Successful implementation of the teacher scholar model is dependent upon actions that reform the ways in which faculty evaluation, selection, promotion, recognition, and tenure are now handled. As already suggested, this task is monumental.

The complexity of this change initiative is further compounded by the diverse practices used in the nation's colleges and universities. Not only does each campus have its own procedures, but each has distinctive features built around unique characteristics. On some campuses, literally hundreds of individuals are involved in this process while on smaller campuses one or two persons might carry the entire burden. Campus governance processes further extend the structure and often slow and dilute substantive change. Finally, the individual nature of faculty relationships within the institution place heavy demands on administrators for individual meetings that place a heavy drain on their energy levels.

Actions taken in support of teaching excellence in this setting may be expressed in a variety of ways, such as taking a strong position in a campus debate, through the issuance of a written statement, or on an informal basis in a group or individual conference. Clearly, the complexity of this challenge requires multiple actions. Academic administrators devote a large portion of their time and energy to personnel items. Whenever possible, the level of attention given to teaching must be enhanced. Theoretically, an administrator could say that all of his or her time is devoted to improving instructional effectiveness. While this may be true, in reality much of the time is devoted to human relations. These differences in perception may explain why administrators sense a strong commitment to the use of employment practices to enhance teaching effectiveness, while at the same time faculty members typically cite this area as the one that requires the greatest level of improvement on the part of administrators. Regardless of the perception, the opportunity for improvement is substantial. The challenge for academic leaders is to extend the ways in which outstanding teaching is emphasized, evaluated on a periodic basis, used as major criterion for promotion, rewarded in a substantial fashion, and promoted on an institutional basis.

Table 3, again, summarizes the views of the chief academic officers on these types of employment-related issues. Not only did this grouping receive the highest ratings by these leaders, it also had the three highest ranked items-- evaluating teaching by students, evaluating teaching for tenure, and evaluating teaching for promotion. These findings are particularly noteworthy since they are contrary to the views expressed by large numbers of faculty members that "teaching does not count for much." These differences may suggest that the fundamental structures are in place, but their application is in need of major improvement. Regardless of one's position, changes in faculty assessment and evaluation must be the leading reform force if a new level of emphasis on teaching is to be successfully implemented. Other actions that might be used in this effort are offered on pages 152-156.

Table 3
Perceived Commitment of Employment Policies and Practices in Support of Instructional Effectiveness (5:71)

Items	% Rating 1, 2 or 3	Mean	% Rating 8, 9 or 10
Classroom instruction is regularly evaluated by students	2	**9.1**	88
Teaching effectiveness is evaluated as a significant/integral aspect of the tenure process	1	**9.1**	88
Teaching effectiveness is evaluated as a significant/integral aspect of the promotion process	2	**8.9**	86
A faculty member's teaching effectiveness is evaluated as a significant/integral aspect of the initial hiring process	4	**8.0**	70
Teaching recognition programs (grants, awards, etc.) that promote effective teaching are available	14	**7.0**	51

Regardless of one's position, changes in faculty assessment and evaluation must be the leading reform force if a new level of emphasis on teaching is to be successfully implemented.

Periodic Review. The periodic review of instruction is one of the primary ingredients in the formula to ensure effective instruction. Data and information collected on a regular basis directly contribute to self-improvement and evaluation efforts. As suggested by Table 3, student evaluation of instruction makes an important contribution to both of these processes. When combined with a variety of sources of information documenting the full scope of the instructional process, student input can prove helpful in determining one's overall effectiveness.

As simple as this may seem, the academy has not effectively built structures that facilitate this process. Periodic review of all faculty is a cornerstone of all instructional activity. Like so many other areas, a series of actions are needed to change current attitudes, perceptions, and practices. These opportunities extend from the introduction of actual changes in the evaluation process to the offering of professional development seminars aimed at educating the faculty about the topic of faculty evaluation.

Tenure Evaluation. The success of the tenure evaluation process is highly dependent upon the original conditions set forth and the actions that transpire during the review cycle. If, for example, little attention is given to teaching in the selection process and in contacts with colleagues, the message soon becomes clear -- "Do what you need to do in the classroom and devote your time to what is really important." The written statements in the tenure policy are vitally important in providing an operational framework for teaching. The actions taken during the tenure review cycle, however, provide the "proof of the pudding." Tenure must be an explicit decision, and the prominence of teaching must be made evident at every critical opportunity. The tenure process requires that the utmost attention be given to the teaching component. It mandates a comprehensive review process. It demands evidence demonstrating the highest of standards. It commands a natural blending of the various domains present in the teacher scholar model. The list of opportunities for reform in this area are almost endless.

Promotion Review. Like tenure, the promotion process is highly dependent upon formal policy statements and the perception of how those statements are implemented. With respect to teaching, promotion means that the faculty member has exceeded the expected norm, has demonstrated teaching success with students, has gained evaluative support from colleagues, has implemented instructional and curricular improvements, and has demonstrated subject matter competence and scholarship. The strength of this process, of course, depends upon a shared obligation by administrators and faculty colleagues to insist on the highest standards possible. Faculty members and administrators alike cannot "pass the buck." If any faculty member is promoted (or tenured) without evidence of strong teaching effectiveness, the responsibility for the substandard action rests with the faculty in the department and the administrative counterparts. Both groups must accept the obligation to evaluate teaching if it is to be elevated to its rightful place. The development of clear statements that delineate the role of teaching on campus and strong, consistent administrative stands on high standards are critical to the elevation of the importance of teaching excellence.

Faculty Selection. The evaluation of teaching competency has been a fundamentally weak link in the faculty selection process. In recent years it has been more common to require prospective faculty members to lead a teaching session on campus, present video tapes of past performance, provide student evaluative data, submit peer and self-evaluative information, and share examples of instructional materials and curricular activities. For the most part, however, these efforts have emerged randomly on campuses and leave much to be desired. Similarly, little attention is typically given to the interview process itself. Here candidates might be asked to respond to a series of questions such as: How would you describe your philosophy of teaching? How would you characterize your teaching style? What use of student data have you made to improve your teaching? What professional development activities have you attended that focus on teaching? What new instructional techniques have you recently employed? How do you systematically integrate your scholarship into your instructional strategies?

Efforts to heighten the attention given to teaching in the faculty selection process make a clear statement to new hires. It also elevates the importance of teaching in the minds of existing faculty colleagues. The expression of the same level of concern for part-time faculty members also may be used to emphasize the importance of teaching. The development of guides, handbooks, and evaluation techniques can go a long way in emphasizing the importance of quality in the classroom.

Teaching Recognition. Tenure, promotion, and merit considerations provide numerous opportunities to strengthen the commitments made to teaching in the various reward structures. As suggested by the responses summarized in Table 3, the various campus recognition programs provide an even greater level of opportunity for reform. With only 51 percent of the chief academic officers indicating that this is an effective area, this may be an item targeted for early reform. The ease with which change can be made in this area may also be a good reason why it might initially get more attention.

As various change initiatives are developed, it is important that support structures are developed in a credible manner, data collection procedures are effectively utilized, and shared decision-making policies are developed. There is no reason to give detractors reasons to second guess the process because of arbitrary actions. Gaining a better balance in the level and types of recognitions can be an effective process as long as it progresses in a routine fashion.

Administrative and faculty leaders must assess their campus to determine the starting point. They must come to agreement on objectives to be achieved, steps to be taken, and guidelines to be followed.

The entire gamut of employment-related processes represents the most tangible arena where academic leaders can shore up the weak underpinnings of teaching. At each step where a personnel decision is made (hiring, promotion, tenure, merit, etc.), leaders have an opportunity to stress the importance of teaching. Teaching competence can be measured far more effectively in the initial hiring stage. Annual review procedures can incorporate in a more substantial way assessments of teaching and scholarly competence. Promotion, tenure, and recognition processes afford countless opportunities for reinforcing the significance of effective instruction. Administrative and faculty leaders must assess their campuses to determine the starting point. They must come to agreement on objectives to be achieved, steps to be taken, and guidelines to be followed.

Strategic Administrative Actions

There is no question that those areas dealing with faculty evaluation and the various reward structures have the greatest potential for promoting the implementation of a teacher scholar framework. The policies and procedures that interface these areas require a high degree of faculty and administrative interaction. While clearly important to the successful implementation of other actions, such a close partnership is not as essential when it comes to a series of supportive actions. It is essential, however, that administrators (particularly chief executive and academic officers) assume a prominent leadership role in promoting the teaching function in as many different manners as possible.

This area presents unmatched flexibility for the creative leader willing to utilize personal initiatives and innovative efforts. While the opportunities for action are endless, strategic actions that support or promote teaching do not happen spontaneously on a regular basis. They require sustained effort, hard work, and, often, calculated planning to ensure their effectiveness.

Strategic actions that support or promote teaching do not happen spontaneously on a regular basis. They require sustained effort, hard work, and, often, calculated planning to ensure their effectiveness.

Strategically planned actions are the easiest way for an administrator to demonstrate a commitment to teaching. Since these actions normally do not impinge on faculty prerogatives or instructional policies, there is an abundance of opportunities that might be used to move the campus. Often, faculty members will positively embrace such initiatives from the administration. They also provide a means to rally supporters and dismiss the eternal pessimists who continue to say, "The administration will never support it! Rhetoric is cheap."

Administrators must go beyond the elementary level of simply making positive statements about the importance of teaching. Strategic actions that foster teaching excellence require an action-oriented commitment. A high level of energy is needed to sustain action over a long period of time. Plans are required that promote the teaching agenda on various fronts. Continuous efforts are needed to ensure that teaching is given high visibility in press releases, research projects, promotional materials, and innovative efforts. Strong positions are required to implement teaching as an integral component in the faculty employment, promotion, tenure, and reward structures. Supportive actions are needed to promote and encourage curriculum development activities that extend beyond traditional departmental interests. The development of sophisticated teaching evaluation strategies requires high levels of administrative support.

Table 4 vividly illustrates the need for substantially more attention on behalf of most chief academic officers. To suggest that there is lots of room for

Table 4
Perceived Commitment of Strategic Administrative Actions in Support of Instructional Effectiveness (5:100)

Items	% Rating 1, 2 or 3	Mean	% Rating 8, 9 or 10
The importance of teaching is emphasized by upper level administrators in speeches and public presentations	3	8.1	73
Academic administrators across campus regularly reinforce the importance of effective teaching	4	7.6	62
News releases and articles are regularly used to focus attention on exciting classroom activities	20	5.8	28
Institutional data on teaching effectiveness are collected and used as a means to improve instruction on campus	28	5.4	23
Research designed to improve the quality of instruction is regularly conducted on campus	42	4.5	14

improvement grossly understates the problem. Other than the typical verbiage supporting teaching, administrators are woefully lax in promoting instructional effectiveness. It is appalling to suggest that there is such a lack of interest in organized efforts to improve instruction. Forty-two percent of the chief academic officers rate the use of research to improve instruction at the lowest levels. With all of its research capability and sophistication, it is amazing that higher education is willing to commit so little to investigating teaching excellence. The opportunities are unlimited. The examples listed on pages 156-159 serve only as a beginning point for the creative campus leader.

Forty-two percent of the chief academic officers rate the use of research to improve instruction at the lowest levels. With all of its research capability and sophistication, it is amazing that higher education is willing to commit so little to teaching excellence.

Teaching Emphasized. The level of visibility given to teaching on campus can have an important bearing on the general perceptions of the faculty. The fact that the chief executive officer regularly singles out the importance of teaching on special occasions can directly influence the attitudes of faculty members. If a dean regularly teaches a class, that can be used to illustrate the significance of teaching. Public statements about an outstanding instructional achievement of a faculty member, a student's success in a contest, or the outstanding teaching record of a department can serve as important indicators that teaching excellence is highly valued and respected.

Also, a regular series of teaching seminars can be used to emphasize instructional effectiveness. Goals and objectives in planning documents can provide direction. Research on student attitudes can be used to suggest overall campus effectiveness. Departmental reviews can be used to gain far-reaching insights into the overall instructional strength of a department. Student outcomes assessment mechanisms can be used to promote the teaching/learning process. Recruitment and promotional brochures can highlight low faculty-student teaching ratios, excellent instructional facilities, student and faculty accomplishments, alumni successes, and other factors indicative of a strong commitment to teaching.

Teaching Reinforced. As suggested, the need for administrators to regularly reinforce teaching excellence remains constant. The ongoing nature of teaching can leave it at the mercy of other pressing agenda and public relations events. Regularly planned actions are needed to remind individuals throughout the institution that excellence in the classroom really matters. For managers outside the academic division, the task of promoting teaching is even more formidable. The demands of getting the job done and "running the office" can easily displace the basic reasons why the institution has established certain policies. Directors across the campus need to find ways in which they too can support the instructional goals of the institution. Giving visible signs to the importance of teaching on a campus often does not happen on a routine basis. Care needs to be taken to make sure classrooms are painted before administrative offices. Classroom functions need to be properly maintained. Academic computer needs should receive special attention.

Teaching Promoted. The tangible ways in which teaching can be promoted are limited only by one's imagination. Like so many other areas, the promotional aspect of emphasizing teaching effectiveness requires a sustained effort. It requires more than an occasional article or paragraph in a recruitment brochure. Those responsible for the production of news releases, articles, and publications need to understand and report the institution's posture on teaching. They need factual information and may require specific instructions on how to emphasize the institution's instructional priority. They need ideas for stories that will strengthen the institution's teaching identity. Specific directions or objectives are needed. The executive leadership team needs to decide what general teaching themes will be emphasized, how they will be promoted, and which data will be utilized.

Promoting teaching can be an effective means of recognizing faculty members for their dedication to excellence in the classroom. Teaching merit award recipients can be highlighted in formal publications and recognition ceremonies. The local newspaper (or in-house publication) might carry a monthly article on one of the outstanding teaching faculty members. New instructional strategies, curriculum initiatives, and classroom research efforts serve as other sources of information that can be used to enhance the level of teaching on campus. Every campus has a long list of teaching successes that may be incorporated into the institution's promotional efforts.

Teaching Analyzed. The findings presented in Table 4 justify the unwillingness of the professoriate to collect and analyze data for the purposes of improving instruction. The assessment of instruction for the purpose of instructional improvement is besieged by many of the same issues raised when teaching evaluations are used for the purposes of a personnel action. When the word evaluation is introduced, "red flags" go up. Instructional improvement must be a continuous process. There is a need to collect student data and other forms of information about instruction on a regular basis. Diagnostic processes need to be established so instruction can be evaluated in an analytical manner, and support systems providing for follow-up consultation and self-improvement need to be implemented.

In addition to individual faculty evaluations, departmental reviews can serve as another source for assessing instructional effectiveness. Outside curriculum consultants can be used to assess the up-to-date nature of the departmental curriculum. National accreditation bodies can often aid in this process. Input from current students and follow-up studies of alumni can add to individual and departmental teaching data bases. While these sources will not likely identify new problems, program evaluations commonly spotlight and facilitate action on matters that need an extra or outside push. Departments can also be the source of important instructional research projects that span several sections of the same course. The need to assess instruction systematically for the purposes of improvement can no longer be ignored.

Teaching Researched. As suggested in earlier chapters, the opportunities to combine teaching and research are unlimited. There are countless ways in which classroom research can be used to advance knowledge, and at the same time improve instruction. Research on teaching in specific disciplines remains as a virtually untapped opportunity for improvement. Research on teaching can serve as a significant means for self-improvement. Department-based research can be used to validate the appropriateness of particular instructional strategies. Cross-departmental projects can be used to promote interdisciplinary activities and assess cross-disciplinary learning gains. For most campuses, the question immediately ahead is where to start in forming a commitment to study college teaching.

Strong administrative leadership is required to stimulate campus-wide initiatives that promote teaching excellence. The professoriate has so obviously neglected this area that it will take carefully calculated efforts to translate plans into action. The agenda must be faced!

The professoriate has so obviously neglected this area that it will take carefully calculated efforts to translate plans into action.

Instructional Enhancement Efforts

In contrast to some of the more strategic initiatives, the use of released time assignments, funding for conferences and workshops, and direct interventions into the natural campus life can provide tangible signs of support for teaching. Such actions elevate the amount of attention given to instructionally-related activities and stimulate others to pursue additional efforts. When a faculty member or department is recognized for a significant instructional improvement or curricular advancement, others take notice. When a colleague receives a special institutional grant or stipend to experiment with a new teaching technique, interest is generated in other segments of the campus. When released time is allocated for an instructional improvement project, a significant symbol is communicated to the rest of the campus.

Often the resources needed to implement actions of this type are quite limited. They can, however, produce multiple impacts and greatly enhance general perceptions and attitudes about the importance of instruction. Such actions may encourage a particular individual to move forward, as well as demonstrate administrative commitment to the rest of the campus. These actions can generate new levels of creative thought among colleagues for activities they might undertake. Even small resource allocations can rekindle the intellectual vitality so essential to the wellbeing of the faculty. Special recognitions can provide avenues and opportunities for administrators to visibly connect scholarship and teaching. And, most important, commitments made to instructional enhancement efforts serve as a direct means to improve instruction.

There are four general guides that might be followed to ensure that instructional enhancement efforts are successfully accomplished. First, teaching must be granted equal status with existing programs designed to enhance the research and scholarly competence of the faculty. Existing programs need to be modified to facilitate a stronger commitment to teaching excellence. For example, sabbatical leave programs need to be available to improve teaching as well as scholarship. Second, there needs to be a balanced commitment to teaching and scholarship. Each institution must, of course, determine what the proper balance will be. This proper balance should not be interpreted as meaning equal dollars, for in the vast majority of cases, the portion of funds needed to support the teaching function will greatly exceed those needed for the research function. Third, no single approach can be used to meet all of the instructional needs of the faculty. Programs need to include a broad array of enhancement approaches that encourage curricular change, instructional innovation, classroom experimentation, instructional improvement, assessment and evaluation, student success and learning, etc. Fourth, a high level of visibility must be given to the enhancement efforts. The importance of teaching can get lost in the "events of the campus." Some academicians have an amazing propensity to lose sight of the positive and dwell on the negative. A high level of visibility must be afforded these actions.

The importance of teaching can get lost in the "events of the campus." Some academicians have an amazing propensity to lose sight of the positive and dwell on the negative. A high level of visibility must be afforded these actions.

Table 5 vividly illustrates that there is a tremendous opportunity for expanded campus activity. As a group, only the instructional development items (described in the next section) received lower composite ratings. Clearly, there

Table 5
Perceived Commitment of Instructional Enhancement Efforts in Support of Instructional Effectiveness (5:120)

Items	% Rating 1, 2 or 3	Mean	% Rating 8, 9 or 10
Funds are available to support instructional improvement items (e.g., conferences on instructional effectiveness, faculty development activities, and other instructional improvement items)	10	**7.0**	49
Curriculum development activities are given high visibility to illustrate their importance	13	**6.5**	40
Administrators regularly emphasize the ways research and scholarly activity can be used to promote teaching	17	**6.1**	34
Released time and financial awards are used to promote teaching improvement	20	**6.0**	33
Librarians are used to promote effective instruction on campus	28	**5.4**	26

is a need for massive improvement. None of the items achieved a good/excellent rating from a majority of the chief academic officers. Furthermore, most of these items do not represent politically sensitive or emotionally-charged areas. Efforts in this area can be initiated without a massive investment of time. Also, these items suggest prime areas where significant inroads can be made with a limited amount of new resources. Faculty interested in making changes can be cultivated, instructional advancement can be stimulated, and renewed vigor can be brought to the campus through expanded efforts in this area. The examples listed on pages 160-162 provide a starting point.

Instructional Improvement Support. The provision of funds to encourage ongoing instructional enhancement activities is the most common and frequently used form of instructional improvement support. Most institutions set aside at least a small portion of funds to support faculty development activities that promote instructional effectiveness. Even a modest allocation of funds to support activities in this area can have a significant impact on faculty attitudes. Small grants or awards can demonstrate an action-oriented philosophy that responds directly to faculty requests. While many projects are often highly successful, the very fact that improvement projects are supported may be more important than any specific instructional benefit. On a long-term basis, however, such actions can have a tangible influence on the improvement of instruction on campus. There are several lessons that can be learned from those campuses that have developed successful programs in this area.

Curriculum Development Activities. Curriculum development activities are a critically important part of the instructional continuum. Much of the responsibility, of course, rests with the faculty who have the primary obligation for curriculum development and implementation. There are several ways in which the curricular agenda can be kept before the campus. For example, outside consultants can be brought in to validate faculty efforts. Disciplinary accreditation teams can be used to review curriculum requirements. Departmental reviews provide still another source to ensure the up-to-date nature and quality of the program. These activities, along with the regular faculty efforts to revise courses, provide a context for the ongoing maintenance of high quality programs. Each one of these activities can serve as an event to reinforce positively. Campus leaders need to continually find means to give attention to the curricular process.

Scholarly Reinforcement of Teaching. One of the potential pitfalls of major efforts to elevate the importance of teaching is the perception that if teaching is stressed, somehow scholarship is no longer important. Obviously, this is not the case. First-rate scholarship is a requirement for all faculty members. It does not, however, need to be defined by the narrow prescriptions of the past. Faculty members can display some aspects of their intellectual vitality through the demonstration of outstanding instructional competence, the development of new instructional materials, the integration of current concepts from the disciplines, and the assessment of student learning. When classroom research strategies are combined in this setting with other outside scholarly activities, the false dichotomy between scholarship and instruction begins to diminish. Faculty members are thereby freed from the traditional "either/or" philosophy and can focus on their primary instructional responsibilities.

Every administrator needs to delineate clearly his/her own personal perceptions of the relationships between scholarship and teaching before any formal action can be contemplated. This intellectual exercise may result in a rough statement that matches the institutional mission and articulates well with campus programs. Regardless of how one might chose to accomplish this goal, strong leadership will be an essential requirement.

First-rate scholarship is a requirement for all faculty members. It does not, however, need to be defined by the narrow prescriptions of the past.

Released Time and Rewards. It has long been common practice on many campuses that faculty members were not granted released time for the purposes of instructional development. Typically, the academic vice president would simply deny such requests on the grounds that such activities were part of one's normal load and should be done without special compensation. (This is an interesting perspective when compared to the rationale for awarding released time for research activities.) While some of the former rationale may still be intact, the use of released time for instructional development purposes has increased rapidly over the last decade. The reason for this shift in philosophy is easy to understand. First, the expertise required to develop some courses places immense burdens on some faculty members. Second, the rapidity of the change process in some disciplines places disproportionate burdens on faculty members. Third, the interdisciplinary nature of many courses exceeds the normal limits of most faculty members. Besides, the "teaming-up" with another colleague usually requires extraordinary effort. Fourth, teaching specialists demand the same level of support as their research-oriented colleagues.

Librarian Support of Instruction. One of the primary responsibilities of the chief academic officer is to maximize the use of institutional resources in support of the educational mission. While librarians typically provide integral academic support in this process, they are commonly under-utilized as an instructional resource. Present-day librarians can do more than simply help students increase their library skills. Many are skilled individuals capable of custom designing course materials and serving as guest lecturers for classes focusing on general or specific research strategies. Others can produce custom-tailored bibliographies. Still others are computer and instructional specialists with capabilities that greatly exceed those of many faculty members. For all practical purposes, the library stands as a major untapped resource in campus efforts to improve its instructional effectiveness.

Each of these opportunities suggests that there is a need for more active leadership in those areas that encourage and foster instructional improvement. Administrators need not interject themselves into the actual curricular process, but bold leadership is needed. Aggressive stands need to be taken on curriculum reform. Direct, tangible support needs to be given to innovative, interdisciplinary, and other program development activities. Strong leadership is needed in the area of program review. Through multiple efforts, the instructional vitality of the campus can be stimulated.

Administrators need not interject themselves into the actual curricular process, but bold leadership is needed. . . . Through multiple efforts, the instructional vitality of the campus can be stimulated.

Instructional Development Activities

Instructional development activities perform a vital role in efforts to shape the instructional character of a campus. Such activities can build a high level of ownership among the faculty. Planned activities can provide visible identity for teaching on campus. Locally sponsored seminars, workshops, and conferences can be tailored to specific needs and are often more meaningful as they are tied directly to the campus. Such campus-based activities are almost always aimed at the improvement of instruction. They provide an open environment which frees faculty members from the threatening nature of program reviews and permits them to focus on instructional improvement. Further, colleagues can often work at this level on a personal basis to deal with difficult problems.

Each campus must make its own decision as to whether its instructional improvement goals are best achieved through a center, office, committee, part-time faculty assignment, or some combination of these efforts. Regardless of the approach, faculty involvement is critical to the successful operation of the instructional development activity. Faculty can create a sense of ownership and build a program that serves faculty needs. Faculty participation also helps counter the perception that traveling experts, technological aids, systems engineers, or even money can provide panaceas for teaching. The improvement of teaching is a responsibility shared by all faculty members.

Without question, instructional development activities present an unlimited set of opportunities for the campus to demonstrate its commitment to teaching excellence.

Nationwide, chief academic officers ranked this area as the lowest among the five categories studied. Table 6 illustrates the low level of support for each of the surveyed items. Less than one third of the chief academic officers awarded good/excellent ratings to items in this area, while a large segment expressed considerable dissatisfaction. There are, however, significantly higher perceived levels of instructional development activity underway in some larger institutions. Without question, instructional development activities present an unlimited

Table 6
Perceived Commitment of Instructional Development Activities in Support of Instructional Effectiveness (5:144)

Items	% Rating 1, 2 or 3	Mean	% Rating 8, 9 or 10
Faculty seminars, workshops and conferences on teaching and learning are conducted on campus	23	**5.8**	31
The campus maintains various colleague support mechanisms (mentors, chairperson, monitoring, etc.) to promote and support effective instruction	21	**5.8**	30
Seminars/workshops on teaching are held for graduate teaching assistants	33	**5.3**	27
Effective instruction is promoted by an organized unit or program (e.g., center for teaching & learning)	36	**5.2**	29
Workshops/seminars on effective instruction are conducted for new full-time faculty members	42	**4.7**	20

set of opportunities for the campus to demonstrate its commitment to teaching excellence. Again, a set of typical actions are listed on pages 163-165 in the Workshop Supplement.

Campus-Sponsored Activities. Campus-sponsored seminars, workshops, and conferences are used to address a broad range of topics related to teaching and learning. They may focus specifically on teaching, have a disciplinary orientation, or revolve around a campus theme like writing-across-the-curriculum or global perspectives. Similarly, the type of initiative may be narrow or broad in its appeal. For example, many committees have successfully established "brown bag lunches" or other types of informal grass-roots programs to get faculty thinking and talking about good teaching. Such programs tend to attract the interest of a small group of highly motivated faculty who can play a valuable role in supporting other instructional efforts. Others may take the form of a series on university teaching or a newsletter on teaching excellence. Campus-based programs serve as an important, low-cost vehicle to stimulate interest, build faculty ownership, and address real campus problems.

Colleague Support Activities. While not as visible as campus-sponsored activities, departmentally-based colleague support mechanisms can provide a strong base for individualized attention. Often these programs are operated on an informal, individual basis and receive little recognition. Many department chairpersons simply assume this responsibility or assign it to a respected colleague in the department. In other cases, more structured programs have been developed. Whether these activities are formal or informal, voluntary or required, the low level of campus activity in this area reveals the high level of potential to increase the level of emphasis on teaching with little increase in funding. Faculty peers have numerous opportunities to assist their colleagues in improving as teachers. Such activities are typically non-threatening and can be used as an effective means to start the instructional improvement process.

Workshops for Teaching Assistants. Increased interest has been sparked in recent years for the provision of workshops for graduate teaching assistants. Pressures from legislators and parents, along with institutional initiatives, have elevated the importance of this area at many institutions. The increasing number of international graduate students has also forced some institutions to accommodate their needs. While these early efforts are noteworthy, most training sessions are largely cosmetic and only touch upon some of the most elementary instructional concepts. Sometimes the workshops are voluntary. There are tremendous opportunities for department or college planned sessions conducted both prior to the beginning of the term and throughout the school year. Again, the room for improvement is enormous. The whole question of graduate education on teaching methodology and evaluation at the doctoral level remains unattended! Unfortunately, significant change at this level will likely come only from institutions that employ such individuals.

Organized Unit or Center. One of the issues that every campus needs to address is the type of organizational mechanism that will be used to support the instructional development activities of the campus. Again, the approach will vary according to institutional intent. Regardless, clear statements need to be made regarding purposes, budgets, reporting channels, and other routine administrative details. Those responsible for the initiative need to assume a leadership posture that will facilitate efforts designed to improve the overall effectiveness of the instructional program. Generally, larger institutions have been more active than smaller institutions in utilizing the center approach to foster the overall effort to improve instruction.

Workshops for New Faculty. The last few years have witnessed a dramatic increase in the number of workshops for new faculty members and a shift in emphasis in the planned sessions. Most of the earlier efforts evolved out of a faculty orientation program which focused primarily on the sharing of institutional information to ease the faculty members' transition to campus. In most cases, they were an opportunity to get acquainted, fill out employment forms, learn about benefits, parking, etc., and be welcomed to the campus.

Faculty workshops often still cover some of the routine information, but teaching has become the primary agenda in many programs. Numerous campuses now have week-long workshops which place heavy emphasis on student learning and successful instructional strategies. Most utilize outstanding teachers from the existing faculty. Some now have planned activities that extend this emphasis throughout the academic year.

Individuals across the campus must have a willingness to venture, to pick and choose, and experiment. There is no one initiative that will ensure excellence in the classroom.

As suggested by these many examples, the type of instructional development activities on campus may be highly diverse. Campus leaders need to assess the campus and chart ways in which instructional efforts can be improved. Similarly, the role of faculty colleagues cannot be overlooked. While the administration needs to be supportive of efforts in these areas, they should not control or monitor such activities. A well designed mentoring program or a set of individually arranged colleague experiences might produce results in some areas that would greatly exceed any administratively organized initiative. Complementary actions are needed! Individuals across the campus must have a willingness to venture, to pick and choose, and experiment. There is no one initiative that will ensure excellence in the classroom. Regardless of the area or the action being pursued, campus leaders must assume an aggressive leadership posture. Only through sustained effort will the level of teaching be elevated to its rightful role. The five identified areas suggest a broad array of opportunities that might be pursued in a low-cost manner. These efforts, however, require a planned set of joint efforts sponsored by both faculty members and administrators. Any differences must be set aside so the goal to elevate the importance of teaching excellence can remain foremost.

Campus leaders must assume an aggressive leadership posture. Only through sustained effort will the level of teaching be elevated to its rightful role.

CHAPTER 8

LEADING THE TRANSITION

The leadership challenge to reestablish the importance of teaching demands more than simply making minor adaptations or "tinkering" with the system. The massive reform efforts require bold leadership that impinges on every segment of the academy. This task is not one of dismantling the present research complex that has emerged as a major strength of American higher education. Nor is it designed to place research in a second-rate role or to suggest that the service function should become an inconsequential faculty responsibility. Rather, the agenda ahead is to develop new assumptions, policies, and procedures that will elevate the role of teaching on campus.

The teacher scholar model and the various relationships existing between teaching, scholarship, content, and learning clearly indicate that the questions ahead do not present an "either/or" proposition. A high level of instructional excellence is an expectation of each member of the professoriate. Individuals cannot be excluded from this requirement; they must demonstrate that they are effectively fulfilling their responsibilities. The groundwork has been completed. It is now incumbent upon campus leaders to seize the opportunity to restore teaching to its rightful role. Clearly, the challenges are great. Reversing the ever-growing research trends will be more difficult than starting anew. Normal day-to-day demands may drain leaders emotionally and leave little time and energy for this initiative. The rewards will be few and the process will be slow, but the future demands reform. Substantive leadership must come from individuals within the academy.

Making the profession of teaching the first obligation of college faculty members suggests a totally new orientation for instructional excellence. It mandates reform in the way in which professionals are introduced to teaching in

A high level of instructional excellence is an expectation of each member of the professoriate. Individuals can not be excluded from this requirement; they must demonstrate that they are effectively fulfilling their responsibilities. . . . Substantive leadership must come from individuals within the academy.

their doctoral programs. It escalates the faculty renewal and evaluation trends already underway. It challenges the reward systems that consistently give greater lip service than cash to teaching. It reaffirms the needs of the profession to regulate itself by evaluating classroom and disciplinary competence.

These obligations are shared by the entire academic community. Students need to insist on quality instruction and push for accountability measures that demonstrate effectiveness in the classroom. Faculty members need to press forward in efforts to ensure the effective evaluation, recognition, and reward of teaching excellence. Departments need to set aside "back scratching" tendencies and vigorously promote outstanding instruction. Committees that have hamstrung genuine curriculum development activities need to be recharged. Policies to promote more effective teaching need to be revised or updated by teams of administrators and faculty members. Department chairpersons need to assume expanded leadership roles in the overall pursuit of excellence. Deans need to assure faculty members that their actions will produce tangible results.

While this change initiative is a shared responsibility, a major leadership role is thrust upon the nation's chief academic and executive officers. Faculty members need to be reassured by these individuals that this is not another log-rolling exercise and that their actions will be supported. Signs of strong leadership must be demonstrated so faculty members will join the movement. Leadership that bonds faculty and administrative efforts into a united front must be forthcoming. Administrators must be willing to support teacher-scholar activity, promote new teaching initiatives, and create imaginative ways to enhance teaching and learning. They must foster an attitude that stimulates the development of a quality teaching environment. Actions need to be taken that reduce the faculty's fear of evaluation.

Campus leaders must assimilate these challenges and act prudently. They must be willing to access current opportunities, develop plans of action, guide the evolutionary change process, and propose new alternatives. While each campus will have its own agenda and means to initiate the essential changes, there are three substantive issues that need to be addressed. First, experience suggests that change of this magnitude is best handled by following a set of basic principles. Second, the responsibilities for achieving these goals are best accomplished through a process of shared leadership. Third, there are several leadership challenges that must be addressed to create a campus environment conducive to the implementation of a teacher scholar model. These areas are the focus of this chapter.

Making the profession of teaching the first obligation of college faculty members suggests a totally new orientation for instructional excellence. . . . Leadership that bonds faculty and administrative efforts into a united front must be forthcoming.

Guiding Principles for Change

The topic of how to institute change is one that has generated widely varying opinion. There is a preponderance of literature on "how to," "techniques to," "helpful hints," "pitfalls to avoid," "do's and don'ts," and "approaches to." All of these, of course, have some merit, particularly when applied to a particular situation. The challenges already outlined require more than an astute application of these suggestions. Beyond these simplistic approaches to change is a set of fundamental principles that connect the basic ingredients in the teacher scholar model with the massive reform needs of higher eduction. These principles are not absolute. They are not independent or isolated functions. Nor are they professed as the ultimate approach in how to implement change on a specific campus. In some ways they may be seen as a simple reiteration of many of the concepts already proposed. Regardless of the interpretation, the eight principles that follow suggest a process by which campus leaders can move forward in their efforts to acknowledge the importance of teaching and to evaluate faculty performance on the basis of the four domains of the teacher scholar model.

- Establish Teaching as a Priority
- Define the Teacher Scholar Concept
- Segment the Instructional Excellence Concept
- Develop a Calculated Plan
- Promote a Team Approach
- Balance the Teaching and Research Commitments
- Expand the Definition of Evaluation
- Develop the Evaluation Process Before Awards

While these principles are not necessarily presented in a sequential order, there are a few key steps that must occur before significant progress can be achieved on campus. As already suggested, establishing teaching as a priority and defining the teacher scholar concept are fundamental issues to the success of any change initiative. Clear definitions and direction are essential.

Establishing teaching as a priority and defining the teacher scholar concept are fundamental issues to the success of any change initiative. Clear definitions and direction are essential.

Establishing Teaching as a Priority. There are numerous ways in which campus leaders can move forward to establish clearly the importance of teaching. Opportunities abound for the priority to be emphasized in mission statements, goals and objectives, and academic program plans. Recognition and reward procedures afford tremendous opportunities to state the importance of teaching. And obviously, the daily actions of administrators and department chairpersons have much to do with the perceptions and attitudes of the faculty about the role of teaching on campus.

Leaders need to do more than pay lip service to the teaching priority; they need to put cash in the hip pocket. It is critical that the promotion and tenure structures reward excellence in teaching in tangible ways. Released time provisions and other means that promote campus-based faculty development activities are most critical. Mentoring programs and other efforts that promote faculty interaction can have a direct bearing on the campus culture and efforts to promote new values and traditions about the significance of teaching excellence.

Leaders need to do more than pay lip service to the teaching priority; they need to put cash in the hip pocket.

Defining the Teacher Scholar Concept. The teacher scholar concept provides a workable framework for campus leaders to build a consensus on the fundamental importance of faculty being current in content and pedagogy. Rather than focusing on the differences between teaching and scholarship, efforts need to be undertaken that demonstrate the various interrelations that exist between the two. Broadening the definition of scholarship and defining the various interrelationships in the teacher scholar model are tasks every campus must undertake. Leaders must articulate institutional values within this context. Campus leaders must capture the multiple sources that draw intellectual energy and instructional excellence into a common framework.

Developing agreement and coming to closure will not be an easy task. But it cannot be ignored, for the evaluative measures that follow must be based on statements that reflect this overall thrust of the campus. They must be built upon common assumptions and reflect a "sense of the campus." With these tenets in place, the campus can then move forward with the implementation stages.

Segment the Instructional Excellence Concept. Instituting a change process that will reestablish the importance of teaching and fully integrate it into the value structures of the academy requires concerted effort on a variety of different fronts. As just indicated, clear definition and direction must be present. The development of a teacher scholar framework and then its translation into operative evaluative structures are the cornerstones of action. The task ahead cannot, however, be accomplished without substantial movement within the entire academic community.

At first pass, this responsibility seems overwhelming. Like all challenges, one must probe beyond the surface tensions to determine what is possible and how it might be achieved. In Chapter 7, five major areas were identified where action could occur. The tentacles of the publish or perish syndrome are interwoven with much of what happens daily on campus. Every action must be viewed as a means to promote instructional excellence. News releases highlight the importance of a new grant, but nothing is said about the innovative instructional strategy being carried out in the particular classroom. New computer purchases are made and major renovations completed, but little is said of their educational consequences. Academic decisions are made daily with only passing reference or consideration to the teaching and learning environment. Efforts must be undertaken across the board so as to support and enhance the ultimate level of importance given to instructional excellence.

The tentacles of the publish or perish syndrome are interwoven with much of what happens daily on campus. Every action must be viewed as a means to promote instructional excellence. . . . The task ahead cannot, however, be accomplished without substantial movement within the entire academic community.

Develop a Calculated Plan. The type of changes already outlined require more than a series of isolated responses. While spontaneous reactions can be used to enhance the change initiative, a total reliance on such opportunities will leave the campus with a sense that the leaders are not committed. Change of this type doesn't just happen; it requires a clear sense of direction, hard work, and constant attention on a series of different fronts.

Obviously, a plan will not ensure success, but the likelihood of success without such efforts is remote. It need not be long and detailed; a few pages might work nicely. While campus leaders may have a sense of accomplishment over the passage of a new policy, these short-term successes must fit within a long-range context. Campus leaders need something tangible that provides directions, that makes connections that may not be so obvious, and facilitates discussion that extends the plan through the addition of detail, dialogue, and discussion. This process, thereby, builds an even greater sense of ownership which serves as a means to promote the change initiative. It creates its own momentum!

Change of this type doesn't just happen; it requires a clear sense of direction, hard work, and constant attention on a series of different fronts. Obviously, a plan will not ensure success, but the likelihood of success without such efforts is remote.

Promote a Team Approach. The implementation of a teacher scholar model won't happen without a concerted effort of individuals throughout the campus. Campus leaders must create an atmosphere that stimulates change, facilitates debate, and encourages action. This cannot be accomplished through a "top down approach" or by relying solely on a "grass roots movement." It is dependent upon the development of a collegial-bonding process that stifles the "we-they mentality" so prevalent on many campuses. The development of a teacher scholar emphasis cannot be based on a set of adversarial relationships. Administrators must open the door and be willing to accept changes. Faculty members need to propose operative solutions that effectively integrate teaching, scholarship, content, and learning. Evaluation models acceptable to both must be created.

These linkages must extend, too, beyond the academic division so other campus administrators can support the planned change. Each vice president needs to consider what actions might be taken to promote the reform plans. For example, public relations staff need to assess media plans to highlight teaching as a theme in news releases. The physical plant director needs to assess classrooms and laboratory plans to ensure they are consistent with academic priorities. Student life personnel need to review their policies to integrate academic goals and priorities into their programming efforts. These campus leaders need to assume a proactive role in terms of promoting teaching. Ensuring that all employees (within reason) have a sense of their role in the teaching/learning process is a campus-wide responsibility.

It is dependent upon the development of a collegial-bonding process that stifles the buck passing scenario so prevalent in the "we-they mentality." The development of a teacher scholar emphasis cannot be based on a set of adversarial relationships.

Balance the Teaching and Research Commitment. Creating a better balance between the commitments made to teaching and the commitments made to research is a tangible way in which the campus can sense a new direction. One need not look far to see visible signs of the importance of research--grant offices are often housed in well furnished complexes in contrast to lessor academic surroundings; research support offices commonly dominate the presence of teaching and learning centers; news releases often promote grant successes but seldom highlight faculty teaching accomplishments; policies provide released time for grant preparation and scholarly pursuit in sabbatical leaves but offer little for program development activities.

Questions of balance need to be addressed. The responses need not result in an allocation of an equal amount of resources, but equity must prevail. The academic love affair with research must at least acknowledge the marriage of teaching and scholarship and the engagement of teaching and learning.

The academic love affair with research must at least acknowledge the marriage of teaching and scholarship and the engagement of teaching and learning.

Expand the Definition of Evaluation. The acceptance of the teacher scholar model demands the establishment of evaluation policies and procedures that translate this conceptual framework into action. Broadening the definition of scholarship is one means. Making the connections between scholarship and classroom content competence is another step. Articulating the relationship between teaching and learning is still another. Each of these areas provides specific examples of where expanded sources of evaluative evidence can be collected.

A brief review of the teaching domain clearly illustrates ways in which evidence may be collected that extends beyond the typical narrow review of student evaluation data. Additional attention might be focused on the assessment of course materials, impact of curricular efforts, measurement of current content competence, assessment of learning, follow-up of graduates, and the use of various measures to evaluate classroom performance. The validation of excellence from a variety of different sources is the only way the full sense of one's professional competence can be measured.

The validation of excellence from a variety of different sources is the only way the full sense of one's professional competence can be measured.

Develop the Evaluation Process Before Rewards. The old chicken and egg dilemma is one that must be set aside before substantive change can occur. Faculty members want assurances that rewards will be forthcoming before action is taken. Similarly, administrators want evidence in hand before new reward structures are instituted. While much of the dilemma may be semantics, it still must be addressed.

The middle ground, of course, results from the mutual respect that is gained through the development of ownership in the change initiative. It is likely that this will require a step-by-step process over several years. Commitments must be made from both faculty and administrative leaders that the results of hours of debate will produce substantive reform. There must be a cash flow at the end of the pipeline!

Commitments must be made from both faculty and administrative leaders that the results of hours of debate will produce substantive reform. There must be a cash flow at the end of the pipeline!

Sharing the Responsibility for Reform

The acceptance of a teacher scholar framework and the installation of the required internal structures necessitate enormous change. As already emphasized, the corresponding needs for leadership are massive. These changes permeate all segments of the academy. They place special demands on academic leaders for almost any one of the agenda already outlined could consume the time and energy of any single administrator or leadership team. Even so, most campuses do not have the luxury of only picking an item or two. A comprehensive approach is required that draws the best the campus has to offer and assimilates it with current thinking throughout the professoriate.

Leaders throughout the nation need to assume the responsibility for penetrating the sacred shields of the academy. Individuals need to demonstrate in a practical manner how to integrate teaching and scholarship, measure content competence, and assess teaching and learning. Models need to be established that evaluate the full range of professional competence. And fundamentally important, campus faculty members and administrators must join together in their efforts to formulate alternative, tangible means to demonstrate that their faculty colleagues are current and up-to-date. This type of movement depends upon a concerted effort that generates action at all levels. Administrators, faculty members, and department chairpersons must assume the major portion of this leadership burden.

Change Agent: Administrative Responsibilities

The normal leadership demands placed on deans, vice presidents, and presidents suggest that a special commitment must be made to implement a teacher scholar model. Without a higher level of dedication, the likelihood of reform is remote. While the critical role performed by these individuals is obvious, their role as change agents must be viewed within a total context. Coordinated team efforts and evolutionary change are essential ingredients in the revolution that must occur. Every administrator must define the specific actions that should be taken within the context of the campus environment. It is obvious, however, that passive or noncommittal stands will not provide a workable

---

Coordinated team efforts and evolutionary change are essential ingredients in the revolution that must occur. . . . Bold, aggressive leadership is needed.

---

framework for campus reform and will likely doom any initiatives that might be forthcoming from the faculty. Bold, aggressive leadership is needed.

Several of the earlier sections, particularly Chapter 7, suggest numerous options that might be pursued. Visible leadership is a critical function that cannot be ignored. Administrators need to find ways in which they can stress the importance of teaching on a regular basis. News releases and speeches provide an important backdrop, but action-oriented activities have a direct and immediate impact on the attitudes of faculty colleagues. The granting of released time to experiment with a teaching innovation can gain immediate attention. Special recognition of a curricular accomplishment or a teaching success can emphasize the importance of other instructional activities.

Administrators who provide a means to support teaching enhancement efforts also elevate the perceived value of teaching. The awarding of teaching grants, giving of mini summer teaching stipends, or the funding of small projects aimed at improving instruction all contribute to the overall goal. While less tangible, strong positions taken by administrators on the development of recognition processes, reward structures, and evaluative efforts are essential to the success of any long-term hope for reform. These "hands on" activities are fundamental requirements of the change agent.

Likewise, upper-level administrators have some unique responsibilities that cannot be forgotten. They need to, for example, find ways to state clearly the importance of teaching. Measures need to be developed that can better describe the educational success and instructional effectiveness of an institution rather than relying on the size of enrollment and the dollar value of grants. Mission statements need to reflect the importance of teaching as do goal statements throughout all other levels. Academic leaders need to expect the support of administrators across the campus. While lip service is often given to these concepts, specific action is seldom found.

Change Agent: Faculty Responsibilities

To serve effectively as change agents, faculty members need to assume an opportunist posture. In some cases, this will mean that heavy leadership burdens are thrust upon them. In other situations, they will need to push and prod administrators to keep the teaching agenda at the forefront. Faculty members will need to form alliances with administrators. They will need to support colleague efforts that elevate the importance of teaching. They will need to pursue ways in which they can support campus initiatives. This active orientation must extend into areas of personal action where direct intervention can shape and influence campus activities.

The pursuit of research on teaching is a prime example of where strong faculty initiatives must be assumed. While administrators can promote such activity, faculty members must assume the responsibility. The design of the research, the use of the data, and the reshaping of the instructional process all fall within the realm of the faculty. The same can be said of the approaches used to integrate scholarship into the classroom. Here again, the measures used to demonstrate content currency must be forthcoming from the faculty in a particular discipline.

For the fundamental changes to be made in the existing structures of the academy, faculty members must assume a primary leadership role. The establishment of evaluation procedures to measure teaching, the development of alternative means to demonstrate professional competence, and the creation of new reward structures all present mandates for change. Reform of this magnitude requires a practical application of the basic tenets of the teacher scholar model. It demands focused attention over a sustained period of time.

For decades the academy has stood behind the facade that teaching could not be evaluated, thereby providing an opportunity for research to be viewed as the most salient measure of effectiveness. There are clear indications and numerous examples that demonstrate the fallacy of this position. Clearly, effective teaching can be measured in a fashion equal to or better than can the value or quality of a research paper, grant, or article. In fact, the amount of evidence that can be accumulated in the instructional process far outweighs what can be collected in the peer review-juried process of evaluating research. Likewise, there are numerous ways in which one's professional competence can be measured. In Chapter 6 a series of examples were suggested. These illustrations provide solid evidence of how "what a professor does can be translated into an evaluative structure." Faculty must, however, come forward to fill leadership ranks. They must be willing to stand before their peers to be

---

For decades the academy has stood behind the facade that teaching could not be evaluated, thereby providing an opportunity for research to be viewed as the most salient measure of effectiveness. There are clear indications and numerous examples that demonstrate the fallacy of this position.

---

evaluated. They need to construct alternative measures of effectiveness and then make professional judgments based upon this evidence. The true success of the reform effort is vested with the professoriate itself.

Faculty must, however, come forward to fill leadership ranks. They must be willing to stand before their peers to be evaluated. They need to construct alternative measures of effectiveness and then make professional judgments based upon this evidence.

Change Agent: Department Chairperson Responsibility

The department chairperson is in a unique position to have a significant influence on the overall success of the change process. While chairpersons often express frustration and ambiguity about their roles, they have latent potential to shape dramatically the way in which the importance of teaching is changed. Department chairpersons can bring administrative insights to bear on the issues, and, at the same time, diminish faculty anxieties.

Because of their role, department chairpersons have numerous direct opportunities to operationalize teaching as a high priority. The transmission of institutional positions on the role and importance of teaching can serve as an important beginning point. Action in this area can serve to establish a context for departmental activity. Formal and informal occasions can be used to extend this theme into regular, ongoing activity--discussing teaching strategies, talking about successes in the classroom, giving advice on how to improve, and listening to problems. Integrating the importance of teaching in the hiring processes, establishing teaching committees, and collecting instructional materials in a resource area are tangible signs of the importance of teaching and learning.

Department chairpersons can bring administrative insights to bear on the issues, and, at the same time, diminish faculty anxieties.

In the normal day-to-day operation of the department, there are several approaches that might be utilized to "regularize" the role of teaching. Student and colleague evaluations and other outside feedback might be shared to celebrate successes and to plan improvements. A mentoring system could be used as a means to improve instruction. This one-on-one approach is often positively received by faculty colleagues. Recognizing departmental activity serves as still another way in which departments can be encouraged to assume a leadership role. Sending interested faculty members to teaching workshops and then using them to lead department efforts can be another way to reinforce the importance of teaching.

Without question, the establishment of alternative measures of professional competence and the development of evaluation measures that validate such competence serve as the ultimate test of departmental leadership. As already suggested, this challenge is shared by all segments of the professoriate who accept the role of change agent. The chairperson can, however, take some positive steps to facilitate this process. For example, the building of trust and acceptance of colleagues visiting each other's classroom can be an important start. Sharing course syllabi, grade distributions, and classroom research and evaluations are all important strategies that might stimulate greater openness. Department curriculum meetings might also serve as a forum where such emphasis might be added.

Providing a sustained level of visibility to the importance of teaching can also be an important part in the change process. The inclusion of related department and campus activities on departmental agenda can serve as important reminders. Enthusiastic support for workshops or conferences on teaching can be helpful. Also, follow-up actions in the form of minutes, announcements, or thank you notes can help reinforce the importance of the instructional mission.

Meeting the Leadership Challenge

The leadership challenges before the professoriate are certainly immense. The needs for reform are obvious. Likewise, it is clear that the required levels of change are dependent upon a systematic, coordinated effort that draws from all segments of the academy. The change process will require prudent action and a willingness to guide an evolutionary process. It will require bold stands, clear vision, and a sense of new direction. Basic questions must be asked and new responses generated. These initiatives must produce a new environment in which teaching and scholarly excellence are seen as joint partners.

Basic questions must be asked and new responses generated. These initiatives must produce a new environment in which teaching and scholarly excellence are seen as joint partners.

The leadership challenge is to create an environment in which the goals of the institution, interests of the faculty, and needs of the students are balanced. Departmental and disciplinary activities appropriately command the primary attention of the faculty. While these interests are understandable, what all too often gets lost in the process is the faculty and institutional commitment to students. Institutional goals can shape some of this activity and publicly promote those activities that demonstrate instructional success. Outstanding teaching can be a means of demonstrating the high priority given to meeting the needs of students. While most institutions meet their basic institutional obligations satisfactorily, they are not always effectively fulfilled. Similarly, the educational needs of the students are sometimes displaced by personal and institutional priorities. Since it is the most basic and sometimes referred to as the most routine function, teaching needs continuous attention. By its very nature, specific efforts are needed to keep teaching in the forefront of the academic community.

The leadership challenge is to create an environment in which institutional prestige is demonstrated by how well students are taught as well as by the quality of research produced. A casual perusal of promotional materials, recruitment booklets, and institutional summaries quickly reveals that research and scholarly activity are the primary missions of many institutions. A somewhat more thorough review of budgets and how institutional leaders spend their time corroborates this perception. The primary function of all institutions, however, is teaching, and it must be so conveyed. Assessment measures need to be developed and used to demonstrate instructional effectiveness. Award and recognition programs need to be used to focus greater attention on the teaching function. Faculty rewards and administrative time allocations need to reflect the balance needed between the teaching and scholarship functions of the institutions.

The leadership challenge is to create an environment in which measures of success and accountability are provided throughout all degree programs. No one measure can be used to demonstrate the overall effectiveness of instruction in a particular classroom or for an entire academic program. Specifically stated goals, objectives, and outcome measures are needed for courses, minors, majors, and the general education program. Such standards are the pillars of the assessment process and can be used to demonstrate success. Academic leaders in the various departments or disciplines must come to agreement on course and program expectations. Measures of success need to be put in place. Institutional efforts need to be implemented to ensure that data are collected and handled in a professional and systematic manner.

The leadership challenge is to create an environment in which regular review and evaluation of all instruction provided by the institution occurs. The systematic review of all instruction is a place in which most institutions have significant weaknesses. Most departments, divisions, and institutions are woefully lacking in their ability to evaluate instruction. When attention is given to evaluation, it is commonly limited to full-time (commonly untenured) faculty members. Institutions must demonstrate their concern for the quality of all instruction. Standards and procedures must be implemented for the evaluation of all instructional staff members (full- or part-time and graduate assistants), regardless of faculty rank or tenure status. Similarly, instruction offered at remote sites must stand the same tests of rigor as instruction offered on campus.

The leadership challenge is to create a teacher scholar framework that is articulated with the faculty evaluation/reward structure. For years, the evaluation of faculty has been primarily related to three major functions of the academy--teaching, research, and service. The teacher scholar concept draws these elements together within a framework of "what faculty members actually do." To establish an effective reward structure requires the collection and organization of evaluative evidence around these basic functions. As the connections become more obvious, the linkages between performance and reward become intertwined in a continuous action feedback cycle.

The leadership challenge is to create an environment in which teaching effectiveness is assessed, evaluated, and improved. The evaluation of instruction has long been the Achilles' heel of higher education. Many faculty members have a negative attitude toward evaluation. Some faculty members have even mistakenly tried to hide behind the facade of academic freedom. The fear of evaluation must be overcome. Evidence of effective teaching needs to be generated so sophisticated reward systems can be implemented. The time has come for faculty members to develop skills in using evaluative materials to improve instruction and to recognize their obligations to be evaluated on the degree to which they fulfill their professional responsibilities. The internal and external demands for accountability must prevail. Simultaneously, instructional development units should be expanded to respond to the growing needs for faculty renewal.

The leadership challenge is to create an environment in which a recognition and reward system that effectively considers the integral nature of scholarship and teaching is supported. Faculty most often cite the failure of the reward system as the reason for the lack of attention given to teaching. While this may be partially true, substantial changes in the reward structure will not be forthcoming until new evaluative approaches are introduced. Data and information are needed that properly assess classroom preparation, organization, and performance as well as content competence. One's teaching competence and subject matter competence cannot be separated. The profession can no longer tolerate the outstanding classroom performer with little or no scholarship or the great scholar with little or no teaching skill.

The leadership challenge is to create an environment in which the multiple functions of teaching, including content, course, curriculum, and instructional development activities, are reviewed. Most approaches to faculty evaluation place emphasis on the actual functions that occur in the classroom. Much of this evaluation is typically limited to the collection of student input. This process needs to be greatly expanded. As a minimum, periodic peer and department chairperson in-class reviews need to be scheduled throughout one's academic career. The review of teaching also needs to be extended to include course preparation, organization and performance; course and curriculum development; and subject matter competence. The assessment of one's scholarship must be incorporated into the evaluation process of the teaching function. The sole reliance on validating scholarship by outside means (e.g., publications and research grants) must be set aside. Internal validation processes of scholarship must be established.

The leadership challenge is to create an environment in which teaching is conceived as an integral component in the doctoral program of all higher education personnel. The graduate school socialization process has long been identified as an insurmountable impediment to the process of elevating the importance of teaching. For more than a decade, articles and chapters have been written on the need to change doctoral programs, but little movement has resulted. This situation can no longer be accepted. Faculty members must be equipped with teaching and research skills. Significant modifications are required for those interested in entering the higher education profession. Assurances must be made that prospective faculty members understand current learning theory, can demonstrate skill in various modes of instruction, can effectively present lessons and prepare examinations, and can design course materials, select readings and laboratory materials, and evaluate student work. Campus leaders must insist on such knowledge and skill as a minimum.

The leadership challenge is to create an environment in which research on teaching in each discipline is stimulated and data to improve instruction are systematically collected. The teaching aspect of most disciplines is severely neglected. Each discipline serves as a legitimate scholarly area in which disciplinary and pedagogical interests could be effectively blended. The modification of regular instructional modes to involve students directly in research activities also serves as a means of combining instruction and research. On an institutional level, the assessment of instructional materials along with the regular collection and use of data on instructional effectiveness can be important ingredients in the overall effort to improve instruction. Changes must be made to integrate these efforts into normal promotion, tenure, and self-improvement processes.

The leadership challenge is to create an environment in which administrators are encouraged to regularly affirm the importance of teaching and to take actions that demonstrate its significance. It is critically important that administrators use every possible occasion to reinforce the significance of teaching. Such actions can be demonstrated by specially designed news releases that promote outstanding teaching among the faculty; through specific references to teaching excellence in speeches, memos, and position papers; and the highlighting of outstanding teaching at various recognition ceremonies. Curricular and instructional development activities can be emphasized. Even the remodeling of a classroom can be effectively used to symbolize the importance of teaching. Teaching deserves special recognition whenever it can be achieved. Of course, formal statements can be made in the application of teaching excellence in promotion, tenure, and other personnel actions.

The leadership challenge is to create an environment in which the campus has assessed the status of teaching and has constructed a plan to strengthen its commitment. Every campus has its own unique character and presents varying opportunities for change. While an increased level of attention placed on teaching will likely draw faculty support, any long-term initiative will require sustained action. Major shifts in attitudes, changes in policies, and modifications in actions do not happen overnight. Likewise, they do not occur without conscious effort. Like any change process, there is a need to assess campus attitudes, review relevant policies, and explore possible alternatives. There is a need to build faculty ownership and to develop administrative support for these efforts. Finally, there is a need to take action in a calculated manner. The plan need not be detailed, but the overall direction of the campus initiatives must be well understood.

The time has come when these leadership challenges must be accepted by the professoriate. While it will not be an easy task to move the higher education establishment toward these ideals, action must be forthcoming. Support will come from many, both within and outside the academy. The detractors and obstacles will be formidable, but campus leaders must step forward in their efforts to guide the process. Leaders must think through the change process so orderly reform can occur. They must provide leadership that creates a new environment. Simply working harder and running faster will not accomplish the desired goals.

Leaders must think through the change process so orderly reform can occur. They must provide leadership that creates a new environment. Simply working harder and running faster will not accomplish the desired goals.

WORKSHOP SUPPLEMENT
ACTION ORIENTED CHANGE INITIATIVES

In the research conducted in 1987 and reported in **Administrative Commitment to Teaching** literally hundreds of ideas were collected on how campus leaders might move forward in their efforts to enhance the teaching/learning environment. These action oriented suggestions are listed in this supplement under the five major headings and the various subheadings found in Chapter 7. Each is an opportunity. The task of campus leaders is to select the right initiatives and determine how far and how fast to move on each venture.

Campus Environment and Culture

Faculty Ownership. Actions might be taken to further enhance the teaching environment activities that:

- **Incorporate course and curriculum development activities as a significant portion of the teaching assessment process** -- review instructional materials in all personnel actions, balance in-class performance with class preparation activities, and assess effectiveness of departmental assessment procedures.

- **Promote the development of policies and procedures that facilitate faculty involvement in critical academic and institutional process** -- utilize academic planning as a primary institutional driving force, maintain integrity in the essential academic procedures, and solicit broad faculty input on institutional initiatives.

- **Stimulate initiatives that promote program, curricular, and instructional changes** -- support curricular innovations, extend curriculum development activities, and promote outcomes assessment approaches.

- **Promote the application of high standards in peer and program reviews**-- exhibit traits of fairness, consistency and rigor, demonstrate an openness to curricular change and innovation, and support initiatives that illustrate the importance of students and their education.

- **Maintain a high level of faculty dialogue in internal governance structures** -- provide opportunity for faculty-based structures to function, utilize existing structures whenever possible, and encourage faculty participate in instructional activities.

Institutional Pride. A conducive teaching/learning atmosphere can be enhanced by actions that:

- **Develop a sense of faculty/staff ownership in the operation of the institution** -- seek broad input into the decision making process, recognize individual contributions in institutional successes, and promote decision making at all levels of the institution.

- **Demonstrate institutional responsiveness to problems and issues that come before the campus** -- assess the various perspectives of an issue, encourage decision making at the appropriate level, and address concerns in a forthright manner.

- **Provide positive working conditions for all groups that foster a sense of self worth and dignity** -- meet with various employee groups whenever possible, promote a customer service student and staff orientation, and maintain "employee sensitive" policies.

- **Establish ongoing mechanisms (internally and externally) that positively promote the quality of the institution** -- utilize measures of academic achievement (faculty and student), incorporate routine activities (program reviews, curricular improvements and personnel changes) into promotional efforts, and give high visibility to accreditation accomplishments, consultant reports, and other outside assessments.

Intellectual Vitality. Institutional leaders need to address these issues in their efforts to elevate the importance of teaching by setting in motion actions that:

- **Set aside the singular approach of evaluating research and publications, and develop alternative mean of demonstrating faculty intellectual vitality** -- assess in-class performance, evaluate instructional materials, assess classroom scholarship, and critique curricular leadership abilities.

- **Create an action-oriented management team dedicated to dealing effectively with campus-wide concerns** -- address volatile issues in a timely fashion, foster a positive working environment for all employees, and maintain an open intellectual environment.

- **Establish and maintain an open communication system that promotes a candid sharing of factual information** -- develop open budgetary processes that encourage faculty participation, respond regularly to concerns based upon faulty or misinformation, and regularly share assessment information about the institution's programs.

- **Support those campus efforts that stimulate outstanding scholarship and classroom excellence** -- promote instructionally based research and experimentation, recognize research and instructional excellence in all forms regardless of how it might appear, and encourage those activities that promote both scholarship and teaching.

Administrative Stability. The implementation of a teacher scholar framework could be enhanced by actions that:

- **Identify and improve those areas that directly affect the immediate teaching environment** -- remodel and upgrade classrooms and laboratories, improve faculty offices, and provide computers and other types of up-to-date equipment.

- **Maintain an open environment that removes procedural barriers, reduces faculty isolation, and promotes academic dialogue** -- use procedures to promote rather than destroy change initiatives, share information widely, and create forms for open debate.

- **Recognize the evolutionary nature of change and the importance of faculty ownership when mounting new initiatives** -- take small steps that improve the environment, utilize faculty-based ideas, and compromise on procedures but not on principles.

- **Provide academic leaders with a clear sense of campus needs and properly inform the campus of administrative expectations** -- issue term appointments (e.g., five years), identify specified sets of expectations, and state planned directions.

- **Establish teaching as the institution's first priority and make appropriate commitments so its status won't waiver or be in dispute with new administrative appointments or academic agendas** -- place strong emphasis on teaching in mission statements, lists of academic objectives, and budget funding priorities.

Administrative Leadership. More specifically, actions are needed that:

- **Provide constant institutional leadership that addresses day-to-day concerns and maintains an orientation directed toward the future** -- establish a mechanism to clearly articulate future plans, communicate institutional positions in a positive manner, and encourage activities that facilitate effective decision making.

- **Support in an extraordinary manner those activities that enhance, expand, and extend the importance of teaching on campus** -- issue position papers or statements that demonstrate institutional positions on teaching, reward (formally and informally) actions that promote effective instruction, and maintain high visibility for instructionally related activities.

- **Build an administrative team with strong competencies in their specialty areas that understands the instructional mission of the institution** -- manage by example, deal effectively with people, and address the service orientation of all employees.

Employment Policies and Practices

Periodic Review. Efforts should be undertaken to:

- **Develop an ongoing evaluative system for all faculty members that effectively integrates in-class evaluations** -- collect and share student evaluation data with appropriate decision makers on a regular and systematic basis, conduct peer in-class evaluations on a semester basis, and complete department chairperson in-class evaluations on an annual basis.

- **Institute comprehensive evaluation systems for all individuals involved in the instructional process** -- evaluate on a regular basis all full-time faculty members regardless of rank or tenure status, review all instruction provided by part-time employees and assess on a regular basis instruction provided by graduate teaching assistants.

- **Establish a regular campus-wide teaching evaluation data system** -- collect common data from all instructional units for comparative and analytical purposes, use separate portions of the system to support self-improvement and personnel evaluation, and individualize a portion of the system to accommodate methodological, content, and other differences in instructional modes.

- **Expand the evaluative process of instruction to include the full range of aspects that contribute to effective instruction** -- assess course development activities and instructional materials, measure in-class instructional performance and the demonstration of content expertise, and assess student learning outcomes.

- **Establish formal means to educate faculty members about the faculty evaluation** -- conduct workshops on how to construct and use evaluative instruments, establish structures that facilitate the improvement of various approaches to instructional evaluation, and provide current research findings on instructional evaluation.

Tenure Evaluation. The critical nature of the tenure process suggests that substantive actions be taken by:

- **Analyzing the actual and perceived role of teaching in the evaluation process** -- review the actual language in the existing policy to ensure that teaching effectiveness receives proper attention, assess the application of teaching components in the tenure process to ensure consistency with the desired goals, and meet with academic leaders across the campus to gain further insights into the perceptions about teaching held by faculty members.

- **Ensuring that tenure is an explicit process that measures specifically delineated teaching expectations and outcomes** -- insist on a thorough application of the prescribed procedures, base decisions about teaching on data and information collected from a variety of sources, and use evaluations collected throughout the tenure review cycle to make judgments about teaching effectiveness.

- **Requiring that teaching evaluations be based on the full range of teaching responsibilities** -- evaluate in-class teaching performance and subject matter competence; review supportive teaching responsibilities, such as advising students, developing course and instructional materials, etc.; and assess the level of class preparation and organization.

- **Initiating a thorough review of existing tenure policies in anticipation of the elimination of the seventy-year-old mandatory retirement law** -- explore various alternatives available to ensure the maintenance of effective instruction, establish regular teaching review cycles (three to five years) for all faculty members, and develop teaching performance objectives for all faculty members.

Promotion Review. To accomplish these goals, again, requires that attention be given to:

- **Establishing threshold levels of teaching excellence that exceed the "departmental average"** -- base promotion decisions on documented teaching evidence that exceeds the norm, collect evidence of teaching excellence from a variety of sources, including students, colleagues, alumni, and administrators, and establish campus-wide levels and measures of acceptable teaching excellence.

- **Developing clear statements and procedures that delineate the role of teaching in the promotion process** -- adopt statements of instructional expectations for campus-wide use, prepare guides to assist faculty members in the effective preparation and documentation of teaching credentials, and state criteria levels for judging teaching performance.

- **Integrating scholarship and subject matter expertise into the teaching assessment process** -- make clear statements regarding the interrelatedness of teaching and scholarship and the purpose of scholarly activity, evaluate the infusion of one's scholarship into the assessment of instructional competence, and promote the use of research to enhance the instructional process.

- **Requiring high levels of teaching competence before consideration is given to scholarship and other promotion criterion areas** -- assess statements on teaching in existing policies to ensure their consistency with state purposes, develop data collection procedures and evaluative approaches to a level commensurate with the importance of teaching, and review on a regular basis the actual application of the criteria in the decision-making process.

Faculty Selection. Teaching effectiveness can be enhanced through a substantial escalation of action aimed at:

- **Evaluating effectively classroom teaching competence during the pre-employment process** -- establish ongoing procedures to assess classroom competencies in a campus presentation during the employment interview, review student evaluations from other institutions, and analyze video tapes and other materials that characterize one's teaching style.

- **Promoting the significance of teaching throughout the faculty recruitment process** -- state the importance of teaching in position descriptions and advertisements, articulate in the interview the role of teaching on campus in terms of promotion, tenure, merit awards, etc., and ensure that the importance of teaching is clearly referred to in descriptive materials about the institution.

- **Assessing the full range of teaching in the selection process** -- assess the candidate's disciplinary competence, measure his/her instructional and curriculum development leadership skills, and evaluate organizational plans and instructional materials used in teaching.

- **Insisting on the demonstration of teaching competence in the employment of all candidates who have recently completed doctoral programs** -- review evidence of teaching knowledge and competence as demonstrated in the doctoral program, require year-long seminars on teaching for full-time individuals entering the college teaching profession, and stress the interrelatedness between scholarship and effective instruction.

- **Establishing standard teaching assessment mechanisms for all part-time teaching faculty members** -- develop short-term (pre-employment and ongoing) seminars and workshops focused on specific teaching techniques; provide instructional guides, outlines, and materials that facilitate effective instruction; and integrate the evaluation of instruction offered by part-time employees into the regular assessment procedures.

Teaching Recognition. Actions are needed to:

- **Establish an instructional evaluative base that supports a diverse teaching recognition program** -- strengthen the commitment to all efforts involved in the teaching evaluation process, utilize existing research to implement new evaluative structures, and collect data from various sources on all aspects of the instructional continuum.

- **Develop internal campus structures that recognize teaching excellence on a par commensurate with its importance** -- reallocate resources to balance support for instructional and curricular development and research and grant activity, recognize individuals who demonstrate outstanding accomplishment in a holistic sense of teaching excellence, and reward individual successes in the defined subcomponents of teaching excellence.

- **Review existing structures to ensure internal consistency in the application of expectations for outstanding teaching** -- maintain high and consistent expectations across all recognition structures, use different rewards to promote achievement in a broad array of areas, and develop both formal and informal mechanisms to promote teaching excellence.

- **Create a proper balance between institutional efforts to promote teaching excellence and other activities (research, athletics, grants, etc.) that are typically associated with institutional pride** -- use assessment data and student/faculty accomplishments to promote teaching; host regular events on undergraduate education, teaching excellence, and general education; and integrate teaching excellence into normal media releases and public relations efforts.

Strategic Administrative Actions

Teaching Emphasized. Campus-wide leadership is needed to:

- **Review all promotional and descriptive materials to ensure that the importance of teaching is conveyed consistently to all campus constituencies** -- maintain a prominent role for teaching in mission and institutional purpose statements and lists of goals and objectives, promote the teaching character of the campus and its overall quality as a learning environment, and use common themes, data and information regarding teaching in all publications.

- **Assess the real and perceived perspectives of the level of commitment made to teaching on the campus** -- determine the level of differences that may exist between perceptions of faculty members and administrators, measure the degree to which levels of commitment expressed by upper administrators are actually implemented, and use follow-up instruments with alumni to determine the overall impact of the teaching/learning environment.

- **Ensure that campus leaders regularly refer to the importance of teaching in their daily actions** -- demonstrate how the integral nature of teaching influences operational decisions, make a special effort to incorporate factual information regarding instruction into regular discussions and presentations, and utilize the importance of teaching as a major rationale for specific actions taken by the administration.

Teaching Reinforced. Campus leaders need to find ways to:

- **Stress to administrators across the campus that each has a responsibility to contribute to the overall teaching environment** -- ensure that personnel policies reference the fundamental purposes of the institution, reinforce actions taken by support personnel to promote effective teaching, and cultivate institutional pride in the performance appraisals of all employees.

- **Ensure that campus initiatives which impinge directly upon teaching take precedence over other projects** -- assess the need to complete classroom remodeling projects prior to office renovations; give priority to instructional data needs over routine administrative needs; and review campus priority systems for printing, computer, and other services to ensure consistency with overall campus objectives.

- **Develop various approaches that stress the importance of teaching to the campus** -- establish a newsletter or regular series of articles that emphasize teaching effectiveness, promote teaching enhancement opportunities and the availability of resources to support teaching, and conduct workshops and host conferences that place additional attention on teaching excellence.

- **Demonstrate the integral nature of teaching and the various functions that occur on campus** -- illustrate the importance of instructional effectiveness for academic personnel and, whenever possible, on decisions affecting non-academic personnel, review budget allocations in terms of their contributions to the instructional effectiveness of the campus, and assess the extent to which instruction is conveyed as an institutional priority.

Teaching Promoted. To place teaching before the public, there is a need for:

- **A formalized plan of action that provides direction for the campus-wide initiative to promote excellent teaching** -- charge public relations and news/media personnel with the specific responsibility to emphasize instructional effectiveness, develop a consistent set of facts/information about teaching excellence, and integrate the instructional effectiveness theme, whenever possible, into the regular promotional effort.

- **Faculty members to assume a leadership role in writing about and presenting their teaching successes** -- promote the development of articles that highlight instructional innovations and experimentation, encourage action-oriented presentations that emphasize teaching excellence and disciplinary competence, and support instructional efforts that provide student involvement in research activities.

- **Concerted efforts that identify people-based and factual-based assessment information about the institution** -- establish means to identify "teaching successes," faculty/student accomplishments, and other items of human interest; collect data through institutional research efforts that demonstrate instructional effectiveness; and review regularly news items to determine how the teaching theme can be introduced.

- **High visibility to be given those items that promote the quality and successes of the institution** -- promote teaching awards, recognition, and accomplishments; use assessment data to promote the basic instructional function; and develop human interest stories from students and alumni that give tribute to instructional successes.

Teaching Analyzed. Campus leaders can promote teaching excellence by:

- **Delineating instructional improvement as a high priority for the institution** -- make a clear distinction between self-improvement and personnel related needs in the campus data collection procedures, elevate the importance of instructional development activities, and reward departmental initiatives that promote instructional improvement.

- **Promoting the development of campus-wide data collection processes that encourage instructional development activities** -- encourage the establishment of procedures that recognize disciplinary variations in instructional methodologies, develop specific statements designed to assess and improve instruction, and design instructional research procedures around the instructional improvement effort.

- **Utilizing a variety of sources to assess and improvement level of instruction provided on campus** -- encourage departments to devise their own initiatives to improve instruction; incorporate teaching assessment as a regular departmental review item; and use consultants, advisory committees, and other outside agencies to improve the quality of the instructional program.

- **Building campus expertise in the instructional improvement process** -- encourage the effective use of data collection procedures, develop faculty ownership in the instructional assessment and development process, and identify individuals on campus who have specific capabilities and responsibilities to assist in the instructional assessment process.

Teaching Researched. Early initiatives are needed to:

- **Improve the knowledge base of faculty members on the findings of research on college teaching** -- create a regular campus-based mechanisms that facilitates the sharing of research findings, encourage faculty members to conduct research in their own disciplines, and take steps to attempt to narrow the gap between general research on college teaching and specific campus efforts.

- **Modify existing structures so they promote higher levels of research on normal teaching activities** -- encourage professional disciplinary associations to assume a more active role in promoting research in the field, review promotion and tenure policies to ensure that research on teaching is identified as a legitimate and desirable scholarly activity, and use rewards and recognition to encourage the development of instructionally-based research.

- **Stimulate research activity as a campus-wide teaching initiative** -- integrate classroom research activities as a regular part of the student's learning experience, encourage experimentation on various instructional strategies, and promote team-teaching experiences that combine successful instructional techniques in one discipline with those of another.

Instructional Enhancement Efforts

Instructional Improvement Support. Special consideration should be given to the need to:

- **Establish a broad-based program that offers far-ranging opportunities designed to improve instruction** -- provide guidelines that are flexible so various alternatives can be pursued, develop faculty opportunities for each of the major instructional development areas, and establish the program through a means that cultivates faculty ownership and involvement.

- **Develop programs and procedures that are responsible to faculty needs** -- limit the amount of "paper work" required to obtain support or participation, place a substantial portion of the responsibility for the program with the faculty, and use the program as a supplement or enhancement to regular planning or budget priorities.

- **Circulate program descriptions, operational budgets, and distribution procedures to faculty on a regular basis** -- describe enhancement opportunities, encourage program use, and highlight program accomplishments.

- **Incorporate instructional enhancement efforts into the regular agenda of the campus** -- fund instructional items of high priority through the use of enhancement funds, utilize faculty members and other local resources in campus-based activities, host and support campus activities as a regular part of the academic calendar of events.

Curriculum Development Activities. The critical nature of the curriculum emphasizes the need to:

- **Assess the level of commitment given to instructional enhancement efforts** -- review accomplishments gained from the existing programs, assess the program in terms of instructional mission and curricular needs, and evaluate the program with respect to the level of support provided for the program.

- **Establish an instructional enhancement program that addresses instructional priorities** -- support the use of curriculum development grants; use enhancement grants to meet the broad range of activities, including daily instructional needs and curricular innovations; and expand faculty development efforts that support instructional development.

- **Emphasize the importance of curriculum development through a broad range of activities** -- establish curriculum assessment and enhancement as a high priority area in the departmental review process, utilize campus public relations and news/media services to promote curricular change, and recognize and reward individual and departmental accomplishments.

Scholarly Reinforcement of Teaching. Steps might be considered to:

- **Develop a position paper on the integral nature of teaching and scholarship or the need for teaching scholars** -- make statements that clearly state institutional directions, encourage classroom and scholarly activity that promotes the integration of the two, and provide numerous examples of ongoing campus activities that illustrate existing efforts upon which to build.

- **Review existing procedures and propose necessary changes that would ensure that sufficient options are available to improve instruction** -- suggest ways in which existing policies (promotion, sabbatical leave, etc.) could be expanded to incorporate the new emphasis on teaching, propose a philosophical statement that could be used to guide personnel actions, and develop new procedures (when necessary) to support the integration of teaching and scholarship.

- **Establish forums to stimulate the philosophical discussion and the application of the teaching scholar concept** -- develop statements of philosophy that can be debated in campus meetings and conferences, encourage academic division/department leaders to develop practical examples of how the concept can be implemented, and study ways to modify existing procedures to integrate the new teaching commitment.

Released Time and Rewards. There is a clear need to:

- **Assess campus practices and develop a program that responds to instructional improvement needs** -- establish statements of principles and guidelines, develop priorities to provide direction for the use of the resources and rewards, and fund the program in a manner consistent with institutional needs.

- **Provide a reward and recognition program that promotes instructional improvement efforts** -- recognize individual initiatives; reward departmental plans and accomplishments; and promote new curricular priorities in departmental areas or campus wide bases for such items as computer-based instruction, internationalizing the curriculum, writing-across-the-curriculum, or other interdisciplinary activities.

- **Review existing faculty personnel policies to ensure that instructional improvement activities are properly recognized** -- assess faculty selection processes, review promotion and tenure policies, and develop new programs to respond to areas not addressed by existing policies.

Librarian Support of Instruction. Significant changes are needed to:

- **Reassess the library regarding its fullest capability to enhance the instructional programs on campus** -- assess the capabilities of the librarians to determine how they can be used to support academic programs, review instructional resources in the library to determine how they can be used more effectively, study bibliographic instruction activities and other library-based services that might be used to strengthen instructional programs.

- **Charge the library director with the responsibility to develop a new instructional statement for the library** -- delineate how the library can become a more significant learning resource, outline ways in which closer liaison relationships can be established between the library and academic departments, and promote ways in which the library can be used to enhance instruction.

- **Establish the library as a fundamental instructional resource for all academic programs** -- utilize librarians on disciplinary-based instructional development teams, assess the existing staffing in the library to determine their effectiveness in addressing campus instructional improvement needs, and use librarians as consultants in the departmental assessment of the up-to-date nature of the bibliographies in existing courses.

Instructional Development Activities

Campus-Sponsored Activities. There is a significant need to:

- **Involve faculty leaders in the creation of a structure that facilitates ongoing instructional development activities** -- develop faculty ownership in the types of programs maintained on campus, establish programs to support campus-wide initiatives and program specific needs, and maintain high visibility for instructional improvement activities.

- **Utilize faculty expertise present on campus to support instructional development activities** -- host conferences to bring local expertise to bear on new campus programs, develop faculty specialists to assist colleagues in other development activities, and build teams of curriculum specialists to assist in addressing campus-wide problems.

- **Provide various mechanisms to support varying instructional development needs across the campus** -- establish a unit to serve as the focal point for campus activity, sponsor workshops on a variety of topics, and support activities across the campus that promote the improvement of instructional activities.

Colleague Support Activities. To more effectively utilize colleague initiative plans should be made to:

- **Establish a faculty mentoring program for all new faculty members** -- demonstrate the institutional priority for instructional improvement; assist colleagues in becoming oriented to academic standards, instructional strategies, and teaching/learning styles; and build faculty instructional teams through the development of cooperative ventures.

- **Encourage academic departments to identify strategies that can be used by colleagues to strengthen teaching in the department** -- develop disciplinary-oriented teaching seminars, use assessment data to improve the institutional program in the department, and assess on an individual basis the effectiveness of various instructional techniques.

- **Establish mechanisms that encourage faculty members to adopt the mentoring concept with other colleagues** -- place a renewed emphasis on self and departmental improvement, support financially modest needs to stimulate colleague assessment, maintain clear distinctions between colleague self-improvement strategies and personnel evaluative efforts.

Workshops for Teaching Assistants. For teaching assistants to be effectively utilized, action is needed to:

- **Develop a list of instructional competencies that must be demonstrated prior to any direct involvement in the classroom** -- require the completion of a regular teaching seminar, develop a hierarchy of skills to be mastered and then phase-in teaching obligations, and add a graduate course on college teaching for all teaching assistants.

- **Establish teaching competencies as a fundamental requirement in the program of all doctoral candidates interested in a career in higher education** -- require teaching and research competencies, provide instruction on teaching and evaluation, and develop skills in course and curricular development.

- **Increase the entry teaching qualifications of all individuals involved in providing college instruction** -- provide campus-based programs to improve instructional competencies, develop modules and micro-teaching components to be completed, and "phase in" individuals on a step-by-step basis who are involved in providing college instruction.

Organized Unit or Center. The need for organized efforts that promote instructional development suggests that actions should be undertaken to:

- **Establish a campus unit that is dedicated to the improvement of instruction** -- state clearly the purpose, objectives, and role of the unit; delineate the expectations for the unit and how it fits within the academic structures; and utilize the unit as a catalyst to promote instructional and curriculum development activities.

- **Provide an adequate level of support for the unit so significant instructional improvements can be achieved** -- establish a physical location for the unit, create staff support with the necessary levels of expertise to operate the program, and fund the program at a level so it can effectively address its objectives.

- **Develop a long-range plan that delineates how the institution will move forward in an expanded manner to address its instructional development needs** -- assess the needs of the campus to determine strengths and weaknesses, identify long-term goals and objectives to guide campus action, and provide an appropriate level of resources to support the stated directions of the unit.

164

Workshops for New Faculty. Some strategies that have been found successful include the need to:

- **Assess the pedagogical competencies of new faculty members and ensure they are properly introduced to the instructional character of the campus** -- maintain flexible programs that emphasize essential instructional strategies, delineate campus instructional priorities and expectations, and present data concerning the characteristics of the student body.

- **Conduct regular workshops for new faculty members that support the instructional needs of the campus** -- maintain a common level of support for the program across all academic units, and focus attention on instructional techniques rather than long-term curriculum development activities.

- **Schedule brief instructional sessions throughout the year that build upon the initial new faculty workshop and extend opportunities throughout the year for all faculty members** -- build programs that serve the needs of all faculty; give specific attention to instructional concerns unique to the campus; and use these workshops to introduce regularly new instructional concepts and more sophisticated instructional teaching, curriculum, assessment, and research topics.

SELECTED BIBLIOGRAPHY

(1) Astin, Alexander W. **Achieving Educational Excellence.** San Francisco: Jossey-Bass Publications, 1985.

(2) Boyer, Ernest L. **Scholarship Reconsidered: Priorities of the Professoriate.** Princeton, N. J.: The Carnegie Foundation for the Advancement of Teaching, 1990.

(3) Boyer, Ernest L. **College: The Undergraduate Experience in America.** New York: Harper & Row Publishers, 1987.

(4) Cheney, Lynne V. **Tyrannical Machines.** Washington, D.C.: National Endowment for the Humanities, 1990.

(5) Cochran, Leslie H. **Administrative Commitment to Teaching.** Cape Girardeau, MO: Step Up, Inc., 1989.

(6) Cross, K. Patricia. "Teachers as Scholars." **AAHE Bulletin** (December 1990), pp. 3-5.

(7) Edgerton, Russell. "The Teaching Initiative." **AAHE Bulletin** (June 1990), pp. 15-18.

(8) Kennedy, Donald. "The Improvement of Teaching." Presented at Stanford University, April 1990.

(9) Nelsen, William C. **Renewal of the Teacher-Scholar.** Washington, D.C.: Association of American Colleges, 1981.

(10) Pattenaude, Richard and Bassis, Michael. "The Role of Scholarship in Serving the Mission of AASCU Institutions." **Defining the Missions of AASCU Institutions.** John W. Bardo, Editor. Washington, D.C.: American Association of State Colleges and Universities, 1990.

(11) Pew Higher Education Research Program. **Policy Perspectives.** Philadelphia: Institute for Research on Higher Education, September 1990.

(12) Seldin, Peter and Associates. **How Administrators Can Improve Teaching.** San Francisco: Jossey-Bass Publishers, 1990.

(13) Seldin, Peter. **The Teaching Portfolio.** Boston, MA: Anker Publishing Company, Inc., 1991.

(14) Smith, Page. **Killing the Spirit.** New York: Viking, 1990.

(15) Soderberg, L. O. "Dominance of Research and Publication." **College Teaching** (Vol. 33, No. 4), 1985, pp. 168-172.

INDEX